Insight Study Guide

Sue Tweg

Hamlet

William Shakespeare

insight

insight

William Shakespeare's Hamlet by Sue Tweg
Insight Study Guide series

Copyright © 2011 Insight Publications Pty Ltd

First published in 2003,
reprinted in 2004, 2010 by
Insight Publications Pty Ltd
ABN 57 005 102 983
89 Wellington Street
St Kilda VIC 3182
Australia
Tel: +61 3 9523 0044
Fax: +61 3 9523 2044
Email: books@insightpublications.com
Website: www.insightpublications.com

This edition published 2011 in the United States of America by
Insight Publications Pty Ltd, Australia.

ISBN-13: 978-1-920693-36-7

Library of Congress Control Number: 2011931341

Cover Design by The Modern Art Production Group
Cover Illustrations by The Modern Art Production Group,
istockphoto® and House Industries
Internal Design by Sarn Potter

Printed in the United States of America by Lightning Source
10 9 8 7 6 5 4 3 2 1

contents

CHARACTER MAP

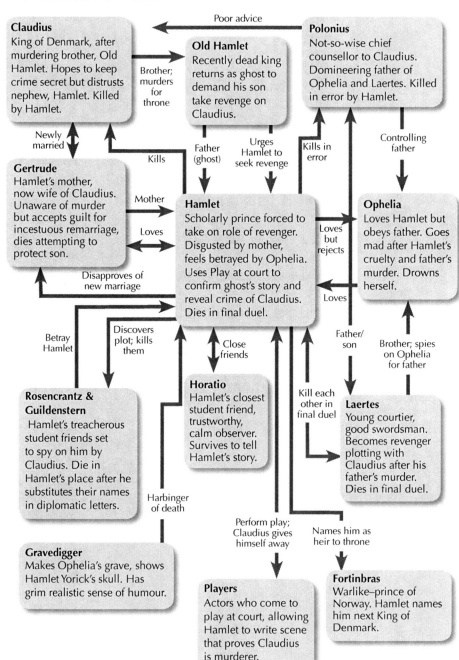

Claudius
King of Denmark, after murdering brother, Old Hamlet. Hopes to keep crime secret but distrusts nephew, Hamlet. Killed by Hamlet.

Old Hamlet
Recently dead king returns as ghost to demand his son take revenge on Claudius.

Polonius
Not-so-wise chief counsellor to Claudius. Domineering father of Ophelia and Laertes. Killed in error by Hamlet.

Poor advice

Brother; murders for throne

Newly married

Gertrude
Hamlet's mother, now wife of Claudius. Unaware of murder but accepts guilt for incestuous remarriage, dies attempting to protect son.

Kills

Father (ghost)

Urges Hamlet to seek revenge

Kills in error

Controlling father

Mother

Loves

Hamlet
Scholarly prince forced to take on role of revenger. Disgusted by mother, feels betrayed by Ophelia. Uses Play at court to confirm ghost's story and reveal crime of Claudius. Dies in final duel.

Loves but rejects

Ophelia
Loves Hamlet but obeys father. Goes mad after Hamlet's cruelty and father's murder. Drowns herself.

Disapproves of new marriage

Loves

Betray Hamlet

Discovers plot; kills them

Close friends

Father/ son

Brother; spies on Ophelia for father

Rosencrantz & Guildenstern
Hamlet's treacherous student friends set to spy on him by Claudius. Die in Hamlet's place after he substitutes their names in diplomatic letters.

Horatio
Hamlet's closest student friend, trustworthy, calm observer. Survives to tell Hamlet's story.

Kill each other in final duel

Laertes
Young courtier, good swordsman. Becomes revenger plotting with Claudius after his father's murder. Dies in final duel.

Harbinger of death

Gravedigger
Makes Ophelia's grave, shows Hamlet Yorick's skull. Has grim realistic sense of humour.

Perform play; Claudius gives himself away

Names him as heir to throne

Players
Actors who come to play at court, allowing Hamlet to write scene that proves Claudius is murderer.

Fortinbras
Warlike–prince of Norway. Hamlet names him next King of Denmark.

INTRODUCTION

Hamlet can seem intimidating because of its acknowledged status as a 'Great Work of Literature'. Forget all about that and just get to know the play — take it seriously but also expect it to be enjoyable. Clive James starts his perceptive and witty discussion of Hamlet's character by describing something he says a lot of people have thought:

> I identify with Hamlet. In my mind's eye he even looks a bit like me. Perhaps a couple of stone lighter, with blonde hair and more of it: one of those rare Aussies who happen to fence quite well and stand first in line to the throne of Denmark. I don't think this is a mad conceit because I think all men and most women who've ever read or seen the play feel that its hero is a reflection of themselves...

This idea of Hamlet somehow being 'like' us is certainly how earlier writers summed up their attraction to the play's complex central character. They thought: 'He's so interesting because he's just as complicated and mixed up and brilliantly intelligent as me. And he's tragic, too!' Someone even wrote an essay asking which interests us more, the prince (character) or the poem (the whole imaginative structure of the play)?

Not everybody gets so excited by Prince Hamlet's wordy agonising any more. The contemporary director Charles Marowitz wrote in the 'Introduction' to his 1960s reworking of the play:

> I despise Hamlet.
>
> He is a slob,
>
> A talker, an analyser, a rationalizer... ...
>
> And how can someone talk so pretty in such a rotten country with the sort of work he's got cut out for him?
>
> You may think he's a sensitive, well-spoken fellow but, frankly, he gives me a pain in the ass.

> Charles Marowitz *Hamlet* (1968)

Over the centuries Shakespeare's *Hamlet* has been edited, reshaped, adapted for film and pirated in many other ways that seem to leave behind little of a 'Revenge Tragedy' that was originally made to please a crowd of demanding Elizabethan citizens standing outdoors, in broad daylight, watching a group of familiar faces performing onstage at the Globe Theatre. It became a theatre classic over the centuries because it was, and still is, a fascinating story about crime and punishment. It is difficult, too, for several reasons, but don't be put off. The language may take effort to understand nowadays but it helps to read aloud so that you get used to hearing rhythms and stresses in speeches, noticing how characters reveal themselves through the words of the text. You also need to know something about Elizabethan ideas on revenge and ghostly apparitions, because they help to drive the plot. You'll find out about contemporary views on acting from Hamlet's interaction with the travelling Players. You'll also realise how many different ways there are to drive a person crazy.

'The play's the thing', as Hamlet says, and this is worth taking seriously. Maybe you'll start to agree with Clive James that Hamlet is a bit like you, even four hundred years on.

A Note on 'Revenger'

In Shakespeare's time the word for someone taking revenge on another was 'revenger'. I have used it throughout this text guide rather than the more recent word 'avenger' as it throws greater emphasis on the act of revenge being pursued by the person directly involved.

CONTEXT & BACKGROUND

When did Shakespeare write *Hamlet*? It isn't known when it was first performed or what the wording of the first version of the play text was really like. It's usually dated around 1600-1, after Shakespeare's *Julius Caesar* had been staged, so that the actors' in-jokes about Polonius playing Brutus could get an extra laugh from the audience, assuming that the same actor in the Globe company played both roles. An earlier version of the Hamlet story by Shakespeare or someone else (known as the *Ur-Hamlet*, meaning the 'prototype') was being seen and written about through the 1590s, although no text of that play survived.

Shakespeare's Reworking of an Old Story

The *Ur* version and Shakespeare's play both used the same history of 'Amleth', a story from Danish chronicles known since the twelfth century that was circulating in European literature, like Belleforest's collection (1570). The Introduction to your edition will fill in this background, or you could look up the original story in Bullough (1973) (see **References & Further Reading**, p.70). Notice what Shakespeare adds and develops to make his source material more interesting dramatically to an audience, particularly by creating opportunities to complicate themes and issues:

- The murder of the king (Old Hamlet) is kept secret at beginning.
- A ghost tells Hamlet about the murder and demands revenge.
- Young revengers Laertes and Fortinbras contrast with Hamlet.
- Ophelia's role is developed, giving her a spectacular mad-scene.
- The Players are created, with a *Mousetrap* play-within-the-play.
- Hamlet dies as he kills Claudius (where the original Amleth lived on as the heroic king and died in battle).
- The historical context is modernised, setting is now Renaissance Europe.

The Text of the Play

Three printed versions of Shakespeare's play exist, dated 1603 (Quarto 1), 1604-5 (Quarto 2) and 1623 (Folio). And all of them present us with a slightly different play.

- Each version is different in line length (over 1000 lines more or less!).
- Whole speeches drop out, or when they appear have different lines in them
- There are different words in key spots. For example: Is Hamlet's 'too too _____ flesh' in 1.2.129 'solid', 'sallied' or 'sullied' in your edition?

- Each text contains odd, unfinished bits of lines where the sense just got lost somehow. Look up these two examples: 1.4.36, 'The dram of eale' bit, or 5.2.195. Notice how your editor has decided to phrase the sentence beginning 'Since no man of aught he leaves…'.

Your study text is a modern editor's compilation, most often based on his or her preferences for a reading of one line or speech over another possibility in Quarto 2 or the Folio version. I chose to work from the **New Cambridge Shakespeare *Hamlet*** edited by Philip Edwards. You're probably reading from another edition, so it won't take you long to spot a few differences between your text and mine, especially in line numbering or wording. Generally speaking, this won't matter for your present study but you should be aware that the 'famous play' known as *Hamlet* is not a polished literary text but was, from the start of its *performance life*, an evolving work for actors that obviously got revised and cut and reworked, with lines misheard or remembered differently.

Hamlet on the Stage

Shakespeare's theatre company, the Lord Chamberlain's Men, had its home base from 1599 at the Globe Theatre, Bankside and played in both outdoor and indoor settings. The company had repeated invitations to play at court for the Queen's annual Christmas revels in the mid to late 1590s. Remember how, at the end of the film *Shakespeare in Love*, Elizabeth is discovered in a public playhouse like the Globe, watching *Romeo and Juliet* (Shakespeare's smash-hit of the mid-1590s). Earlier in the film the players perform *Love's Labours Lost* for her private entertainment at court in a small indoor hall temporarily converted for a show. In 1608, the company was permitted to use its Blackfriars building as a permanent indoor theatre, too.

Richard Burbage, the company's lead actor who played the new role of Hamlet was about thirty years old in 1600. He was an intelligent, athletic actor, who was also a good artist and capable at swordplay. Burbage was a fighting hero type who played the lead in many shows around town, including (possibly) the central revenger in a revival of Kyd's 1580s crowd-pleaser *The Spanish Tragedy*. The names of other possible actors are unknown, although there was a tradition that Shakespeare himself played the ghost. If it's true, I wonder why he chose that part for himself. Was it, perhaps, as a kind of theatrical joke because the ghost initiates the entire tragic action of the play? Without the ghost, Hamlet would just remain a melancholy, disgruntled prince, moping about the frailty of women.

The Play's Concerns and Historical Realities

While it's generally accepted that 'great works of art' can stand alone and, by definition, outlive their original narrow historical period, we shouldn't forget that they inevitably communicate at some level with us about things in life that were once of immediate significance, too. In considering *Hamlet*, I take into account an historical event around 1601 that may have coloured Shakespeare's own imaginative process and affected how at least *some* members of a contemporary audience received his challenging new play about regicide, revenge and the dangers of thinking.

In 1601, the Earl of Essex's rebellion was a sign of growing political instability. By the late 1590s an obvious problem for everyone was that their adored queen was getting old and she had no heir. Within two years she would be dead and the throne would pass to her Scottish nephew, James, giving Shakespeare more food for thought, some of which he expressed in his next tragedy, *Macbeth*. In 1601 the country's mood was unsettled by rumours of assassination attempts and yet another Spanish armada preparing to attack England (after two previous failures in 1588 and 1597).

The young Earl of Essex, Elizabeth's favourite, was tried and executed for high treason in early 1601, following his poor record as a military leader and after an open attempt at rebellion. His grab for power came at the end of several years of insubordinate behaviour to the Queen, with whom he was flirting. Their tension first flared openly in 1598 when Elizabeth slapped his ears at a Council meeting for being cheeky. Shakespeare had connections in Essex's circle of friends and a special revival of his recent play *Richard II* (about the overthrow and murder of a weak ruler) was requested by them for performance at the Globe just before the rebellion attempt occurred.

Elizabeth commented soon afterwards that she knew full well what had been meant by choosing that show — people would identify *her* with Richard II. The play was the thing — as was the new tragedy *Hamlet*, where issues of kingship, regicide, fitness to rule and treachery whirl around the onstage world of Elsinore. Even as innocent players, Shakespeare and company must have felt themselves treading on potentially very dangerous ground for a while. Even though *Richard II* failed to whip up a supportive theatre mob for Essex, audience members must have made their own connections, too.

GENRE, STYLE & STRUCTURE

Genre

Shakespeare created intensely absorbing tragic characters in the plays that take their names: *Hamlet, Macbeth, Othello* and *King Lear*. Many other individual characters, all created before Hamlet, also attain great tragic stature: Romeo, Juliet, Brutus and Shylock. Plays continue to interest us when we can empathise with characters that go beyond being just stage 'types'. Their lives, expressed through their words and actions, have psychological complexity like our own and, therefore, we can understand and identify with them. A similar thing happens when we watch what we'd call a very good film, because we empathise strongly with characters in their situations and care about what will happen to them.

Key Point

Hamlet is a Revenge Tragedy. This means it combines two very powerful dramatic genres into one intense experience for the reader and audience.

1. Tragedy

The very name 'tragedy' derives from an ancient song of the sacrificial goat (*tragos oidos*), appearing in the symbolic form of Greek woodland gods (satyrs associated with unrestrained fertility) and Pan — the god of wild Nature associated with 'panic' (the word derives from Pan). Early ritual theatre, involving regular sacrifices to these gods, evolved into the classical Greek form dedicated to Dionysus, God of disguises, ecstatic liberation ('ecstasy' is the state you're in when you 'stand outside yourself') and intensely mystical theatre experience. Tragedy takes us into dangerous but thrilling psychological territory, where we are led to feel what Aristotle called *catharsis*, a beneficial and uplifting experience for us at the end, after a roller-coaster ride of pity and terror with worthy but flawed characters.

Fundamental ideas about what a tragic play is about, what the characters will be like and how it will turn out come originally from Aristotle. Plot must be central, it's the 'soul' of tragedy. It should include elements like a reversal of fortune for a person who is, significantly, neither all good nor all bad but trips up or miscalculates (*hamartia*), and there should be a moment of recognition, a change from ignorance to knowledge, with a *crisis* (the turning point in the main character's fortunes) leading to the final outcome or *catastrophe*.

In Greek tragedy terrible things occur offstage and then an eyewitness comes on to describe what happened. The mind is powerful at imagining horrors. Roman tragedy took the staging of horrible moments a step further. One playwright, Seneca, had all the violence happen onstage, giving the term 'Senecan' to bloodthirsty moments. Seneca's plays were studied in Elizabethan schools, giving Shakespeare his introduction to a violently expressive form of tragedy.

Features of Hamlet as Shakespearean Tragedy

a) The *catharsis* should be experienced at the end of the play, when Hamlet has finally achieved his goal.

- Do you experience a *catharsis* at the end of the play? Do you feel this is a good conclusion — or the only possible conclusion?

b) Both as readers and audience, we feel different degrees of **pity and terror** for characters as the action unfolds.

- Where do *you* feel most strongly for characters? Locate those moments and note your responses. I know, for example, I feel predominantly terror for Hamlet when he's with the ghost, in the 'closet' scene with Gertrude, just before the final duel begins and during it. I feel pity for him in his first scene, whenever he's with Ophelia (even when he's tormenting her) and the feeling builds with each tormented soliloquy. And I feel overwhelming pity for the villain Claudius as he tries to pray but just can't feel repentant.

c) In Shakespeare's interpretation of *hamartia*, the tragic character usually gives way to a weakness in character or a previously repressed desire, or tries to tough it out in a situation where he/she feels ignorant or vulnerable. Look up 1.4.24, where Hamlet calls this flaw 'some vicious mole of nature'.

- Is Hamlet the only tragic character in the play, a worthy but flawed person? What is his *hamartia*?

d) **Moments of recognition** occur in key scenes for Hamlet, Claudius and Gertrude.

- How does the full truth dawn on Hamlet? It all seems to fall into place for him when the ghost tells his story, but does he have the full picture? I think he gets to an almost Zen awareness only in 5.2.192-5. Claudius hits that moment when he leaps up at the Play (2.2.240). Gertrude recognises her faults in the 'closet' scene (3.4).

e) Look at moments of physical violence in the play, Hamlet with Ophelia and Gertrude (with the murder of Polonius), and the final scene.

- How do you respond to Hamlet's callous mockery of Polonius's body? Also, consider the impact of seeing the last scene in performance as the bodies pile up.

2. Revenge

> When the bad bleeds, then is the tragedy good. Vindice, *The Revenger's Tragedy*, Cyril Tourneur (1607)

Revenge is a kind of wild justice...Certainly, in taking revenge, a man is but even with his enemy; but in passing it over, he is superior; for it is a prince's part to pardon...The more tolerable sort of revenge is for those wrongs which there is no law to remedy...It is certain that a man that studieth revenge keeps his own wounds green, which otherwise would heal and do well...

'Of Revenge' in *Essays*, Francis Bacon (1597)

Do you remember the boy called John Webster in *Shakespeare in Love*? Webster grew up to write a terrifying, sophisticated revenge play called *The Duchess of Malfi* (1623). The main vogue for the Revenge genre was the 1580s and 90s. Kyd's *The Spanish Tragedy* (c.1582-92) was a smash hit, about Hieronymo, a father avenging his son's murder. It set the rules for a grotesque and excessive kind of tragic exploration of the revenge ethic. Shakespeare tried a Roman revenge play in *Titus Andronicus* (1593-4) with multiple execution, rape, mutilation and a final cannibal feast. See the recent film version *Titus* (dir. Julie Taymour) to get an idea of Senecan violence at its most confronting.

Features of the Elizabethan Revenge Play

- A ghost appears to initiate the process and nominate the revenger.
- The revenger protects himself by pretending to be mad.
- The revenger devises a play, or sets up an elaborate masque entertainment at a feast, to nail his enemies.
- Violence occurs onstage — and there's blood.
- Corruption is purged from the state by the act of revenge.

Hamlet incorporates all of the above features into its tragic form. It deliberately takes its time as a story, delaying the resolution the audience anticipates (Hamlet wallowing in Claudius's blood as directed by the ghost) in order to maximise thrills and complicate the ethical dilemmas inherent in the genre.

In fact, *Hamlet* intensifies the audience's concentration on just what revenge is all about by duplicating its process: as Hamlet blunders towards his revenge, he accidentally kills Laertes' father, which leads Laertes to seek revenge on Hamlet. Both revengers reach their destination together in a final duel and succeed in destroying not only their individual targets but also themselves. Two other young male figures, Fortinbras and the fictional 'dramatic character' Pyrrhus, given voice by both Hamlet and the Player (2.2.408+), offer further images of the revenger in action.

Style

Style notices decisions that have been taken about how a play is constructed, the choice of language and its sound, the degree of dignity of characterisation, attention to the unfolding pace of ideas, appropriateness of setting to the seriousness of the theme and so on. The overall style traditionally appropriate to tragedy is noble, serious and poetic. Notice, though, how Shakespeare's language works metaphorically to undermine nobility. Hamlet's belief that 'the time is out of joint' (1.5.189) is reinforced through images of disease and corruption which intensify the sense of a decaying, immoral world falling apart.

Key Point

Hamlet is written in two language styles — blank verse and prose.

1. Prose

Prose is basically the language structure and rhythms of ordinary speech. I'm writing prose now.

Look at 5.1. The gravedigger speaks prose and Hamlet continues the friendly conversation in the same way until Ophelia's funeral arrives, when the language of the scene shifts into blank verse.

Hamlet, the prince who politely speaks verse, isn't talking down to the workman by speaking prose. It signals something more subtle about the equality of the interaction, suggesting a mixture of relaxation and human sharing of something serious. Hamlet's intensely interested in the subject being discussed and the gravedigger isn't just a comic rustic, good for a bit of teasing by a couple of idle noblemen, but a specialist sharing his expert advice.

Hamlet habitually drops into prose with Polonius, Rosencrantz and Guildenstern and the Players (2.2.170+). His conversation with Ophelia in the 'nunnery' scene is in prose, after a start in strained verse from Ophelia that lets us know she's nervous and dissembling (3.1). The 'Play' scene (3.2) is prose until Hamlet's soliloquy at the end and the last scene mixes verse and prose in the turmoil of the fight. Look at each of these scenes carefully.

2. Blank verse

This is basically unrhyming lines of poetry with a discernible bouncing rhythm in the lines of a speech, made up of stressed and unstressed parts of words (syllables). The more you read Shakespeare aloud the more you'll become accustomed to hearing this patterning of five stressed to five unstressed syllables per line (known as **iambic pentameter**). Rhythms can vary, so be alert to shifts in the stress pattern. It doesn't have to be a singsong bounce of la **la** la **la** la **la** la **la** la **la**, in fact, it rarely sounds like that. Occasionally an extra syllable sneaks in, or a stress, or a beat of silence completes the rhythm. It's a matter of attuning your ears to the language pattern and feeling the most natural expression. Study the following lines of **iambic pentameter** with stressed syllables marked in bold as I would say them:

> Though **yet** of **Ham**let our **dear bro**ther's **death**... (What's the effect when 'dear' is emphasised?) **O** what a **ro**gue and **pea**sant **slave** am **I**!

> ('O' stressed is a real groan or sigh of anguish.) My **strong**er **guilt** de**feats** my **strong** intent.

> ('[G]uilt' is made the emphasis on which the line balances.) I **hoped thou should'st** have been **my Ham**let's **wife**.

> ('[T]hou' 'my' loving balance and sad unfulfilled wish in 'should'st'.) **Friends both**, go **join** you with some **further aid**. (Two strong stresses as Claudius rallies support.) **No, no**, the **drink**, the **drink** — O my **dear Ham**let ['let' is extra syllable].

> The **drink**, the **drink** — [silent beat] **I am pois**oned [silent beat, dies].

> (Language disintegrates, stumbles, dying speaker, urgent communication of warning.)

Structure

In modern editions the play is divided into 5 acts and 20 scenes.

Act 1: establishes problem, ghost appears: 'something is rotten in the state of Denmark', Hamlet is seen as reluctant revenger.

Act 2: shows Hamlet in states of madness and introduces the Players.

Act 3: The *Mousetrap* play succeeds, Hamlet fails to kill Claudius, accidentally kills Polonius, Gertrude reformed.

Act 4: Hamlet sent to England, Ophelia's madness/suicide, Claudius plots duel with eager revenger Laertes.

Act 5: Hamlet returns, Ophelia's burial. Emphasis on death, acceptance, 'the readiness is all'. Hamlet, Claudius, Gertrude, Laertes killed. Fortinbras takes over as new king of Denmark.

Importance of Soliloquies

Like arias in opera or solo numbers in musical theatre where we get a chance to look into the very heart of someone's feelings, characters in Shakespeare don't lie — either to us or themselves — when performing a soliloquy, because they assume they're 'alone' with their private thoughts. Audiences accept this convention, understanding that we must take the characters as they are, warts and all, because what they express they genuinely feel. Hamlet has seven crucially important soliloquies, Claudius a very significant one, and Ophelia also a short but poignant one at the end of the 'nunnery' scene. Know them all well enough to quote key lines in support of lots of thematic arguments.

Hamlet's Seven Soliloquies

1   'O that this too too solid flesh would melt…' (1.2.129+)

2   'O all you host of heaven!…' (1.5.92+)

3   'O what a rogue and peasant slave am I…' (2.2.502+)

4   'To be or not to be…' (3.1.56+)

5   'Tis now the very witching time of night…' (3.2.349+)

6   'Now might I do it pat, now a is a-praying…' (3.3.73+)

7   'How all occasions do inform against me…' (4.4.32+)

Ophelia's Soliloquy
'O what a noble mind is here o'erthrown!...' (3.1.144+)

Claudius's Soliloquy
'O my offence is rank, it smells to heaven...' (3.3.36+)

For an example of how to select ideas from Hamlet's soliloquies, turn to the theme **The Relationship between Thought and Action** (pp.59-61) to see how I've modelled a developing line of argument for you.

SCENE-BY-SCENE ANALYSIS

- **Acts and scenes are numbered with Arabic numerals 1, 2, 3, 4, 5 as in the edition I have used.** Some people use Roman or Arabic numerals or a mix throughout, for example, I.1 or 1.i or 1.1. As long as the mix is consistent, it doesn't matter as they all give the same information. Scene divisions are editorial choices in Shakespeare, so you may find that your text differs once or twice from mine.

- **Key Quotations** to memorise are singled out in bold — this is a complex 'quotation-filled' play.

- **Key Scenes** are highlighted.

- **Build character notes as you read**, making your own list of key quotes for each one.

- Collate quotations for character responses to key events or themes. For example, you could trace a main character's responses to Death or Guilt and Responsibility, scene by scene, as the tragedy unfolds.

Act 1

1.1 Elsinore castle. Establishes scene — always important in Shakespeare. This one features a ghost.

Barnardo and Francisco, two soldiers on night guard, frozen with cold and nervous about something, meet to change watch around midnight. The atmosphere of anxiety onstage builds immediately in their short, sharp exchanges. Francisco is glad to be finished for the night. The tense situation is intensified when another pair of watchers joins Barnardo. Horatio, also cold but obviously unafraid and sceptical, has been brought along by another guard, Marcellus, as a scholarly witness to whatever it is the soldiers have been terrified of seeing again, some 'dreaded sight', an 'apparition'. It's important for the audience to recognise Horatio's calm rational approach: he thinks this ghost is the soldiers' 'fantasy', but he's still willing to listen to Barnardo's report.

Suddenly, as the bell tolls the next hour, the ghost of Denmark's recently dead king, Old Hamlet, appears. Horatio's rational ideas are turned upside down. Like the soldiers, he's frightened but tries to 'speak to it' when they urge him. Horatio's trained mind manages to think beyond immediate gut-wrenching terror to wonder *why* the ghost has appeared. He guesses correctly. **'This bodes some strange eruption to our state'** (1.1.69).

His long reply to Marcellus about military preparations conveys important information to the audience about two things. Firstly, the present political turmoil is the result of earlier military events directly involving Old Hamlet. He met king Fortinbras of Norway in a highly risky combat over possession of land, where they agreed beforehand through rules of chivalry that the winner would take all — Hamlet then killed Fortinbras and seized the land. Secondly, Young Fortinbras (the dead king's son, will be important later for young Hamlet) has raised an army to attack Denmark and retrieve the land his father lost. Is the ghost appearing as the pointless feuding is set to continue, as Barnardo thinks?

Horatio knows more than they do about why ghosts walk. It could be an omen of something catastrophic. In any case, **'A mote it is to trouble the mind's eye'** (1.1.112). Horatio's brilliant image (the tiny speck of irritation that lodges in the mind, stimulating speculation) leads him to think of other reported cosmic omens surrounding the assassination of Julius Caesar. While he can't know yet that Old Hamlet was murdered, Horatio makes the first significant tragic link for the audience.

When the ghost reappears, Horatio has conquered his fear and asks it classic questions the Elizabethan audience would associate with unquiet ghosts. Still it refuses to communicate. After it vanishes at dawn, Horatio suggests telling young Hamlet about his father's spirit. Notice how the scene ends with Marcellus's lyrical speech about 'hallowed and gracious' times, underlining the contrast with Denmark's current situation.

Key Scene.

1.2 Danish court. Establishes Hamlet's troubled relationship with mother and uncle.

Claudius, elected king after his brother's death, gives reasons for marriage to Gertrude, his brother's widow. Then, after making sensible diplomatic decisions about Fortinbras and giving Laertes, son of the chief counsellor Polonius, permission to go abroad, he turns his attention to Hamlet, who refuses to be called 'son' by his new uncle-father. Muttering **'A little more than kin and less than kind'** (1.2.65), he's closer kin than he should be and he isn't doing it out of kindness to Hamlet.

Claudius and Gertrude try to talk Hamlet out of his grief. He resists, angry that his mother should think it only **'seems'** special to him (1.2.76-86). He agrees to stay at Court rather than return to university only when his mother asks him, not when Claudius commands. The tension is palpable even though Claudius puts a good spin on 'this gentle and unforced accord of Hamlet'(1.2.123).

SOLILOQUY 1: 'O that this too too solid flesh would melt...' (1.2.129-58)
Alone, Hamlet reveals **'how weary, stale, flat and unprofitable'** (1.2.133) everything in the decaying world seems to him. Less than two months after his father's death his mother has proved how little she cares by remarrying incestuously and her choice of husband revolts him. **'It is not, nor it cannot come to good'** (1.2.158) he believes, but he cannot be openly critical.

The mood lightens slightly when Horatio enters and is greeted warmly as a fellow student and 'my good friend' (1.2.163) by Hamlet. Notice how Hamlet can speak honestly to Horatio, revealing his dismay at the proximity of royal wedding to royal funeral by the wry joke about using leftovers from one feast for the next. Understandably, Horatio reacts to 'My father, methinks I see my father' (1.2.184), then seizes his opportunity to tell Hamlet about the ghost. After close questioning, Hamlet agrees to watch that night with them. Hamlet links tragedy and revenge ideas with **'My father's spirit, in arms! All is not well. / I doubt some foul play'** (1.2.254-5).

1.3 Laertes and Polonius warn Ophelia about trusting Hamlet's love.

As a prince, Hamlet is not free to choose his own partner, argues Laertes, **'for on his choice depends / The sanctity and health of this whole state'** (1.3.20-1). Ophelia listens but, in return, jokingly warns Laertes to heed his own advice about sexual dangers on 'the primrose path of dalliance' (1.3.50).

Polonius (who we realise has overheard the last part of their conversation, eavesdropping as usual) joins his children. After giving Laertes a last blast of long-winded fatherly advice, he subjects Ophelia to intense verbal bullying for being foolishly in love with a prince. Without any evidence to justify his cruel words, he reiterates Laertes' warning about Hamlet, commanding her **'Do not believe his vows'** (1.3.127). Ophelia defends Hamlet's behaviour as 'honourable' but agrees to obey Polonius and avoid further contact with Hamlet.

1.4 On the battlements after midnight, Hamlet and his friends wait for the ghost to appear.

Sounds of loud revelry at the royal feast lead Hamlet to explain that, although Danes have noble qualities, they are seen as drunkards by foreigners.

Key Speech

Hamlet (1.4.23-36): Hamlet speculates aloud about how it's the same with individuals — one particular fault in their character, **'some vicious mole of nature'** (1.4.24), may influence other people to believe they're completely bad and lead to their downfall.

When the ghost appears, Hamlet begins to question it. Despite his friends' attempts to prevent him, he follows the ghost alone. Marcellus comments to Horatio that **'Something is rotten in the state of Denmark'** (1.4.90).

Key Scene

1.5 The ghost of Old Hamlet tells how he was murdered by his own brother, Claudius, 'The serpent that did sting thy father's life / Now wears his crown' (1.5.39-40).

Exhorting Hamlet to **'revenge his foul and most unnatural murder'** (1.5.25), the ghost speaks of incest and adultery, implicating Gertrude, his '**most seeming virtuous queen**' (1.5.46) in the wrong done to him. Worst of all, Old Hamlet explains how he suffers because he was killed when he was in a state of sin, unprepared for death. As dawn begins to break, he leaves Hamlet with the injunction to '**remember** [and] **bear it not**'.

SOLILOQUY 2: 'O all you host of heaven! O earth! what else?...'
(1.5.92-112).

Hamlet's second soliloquy reveals his deep emotional and psychic shock at the ghost's news, especially since it confirms his own vague suspicions. Appalled by his mother, the '**pernicious woman**', and his uncle, the '**smiling damnèd villain**', Hamlet feverishly writes down '**That one may smile and smile and be a villain**' (1.5.108). Even though the ghost warned Hamlet '**Taint not thy mind**' (1.5.85), he is clearly disturbed when his friends find him. Without telling them the whole background revealed to him by his father's ghost, Hamlet demands that they swear to support him if he might, in the future, sometimes '**put an antic disposition on**' (1.5.72), that is, act mad. They agree, and he closes the scene, reiterating his distress that '**The time is out of joint: O cursèd spite / That ever I was born to set it right**' (1.5.189-90).

Act 2

2.1 Polonius shows the audience how deviously 'Machiavellian' he is as a father — but just how wrong he can be in policing his children. First, Polonius instructs Reynaldo precisely how to check on Laertes' behaviour in Paris: he must snoop around his acquaintances and insinuate that Laertes is going a bit wild to see if they agree, and so 'By indirections find directions out' (2.1.64).

When Ophelia enters in distress at Hamlet's apparently 'mad' behaviour towards her, Polonius immediately assumes that '**This is the very ecstasy of love**' (2.1.100). He blames himself for jumping to the wrong conclusion about Hamlet's intentions, since Ophelia's obedient refusal of contact with him has obviously brought on Hamlet's brooding craziness she describes in her long speech (2.1.85-98). Polonius hurries to inform Claudius.

2.2 Long scene of court intrigue; Polonius suggests Hamlet is mad; Hamlet meets and suspects Rosencrantz and Guildenstern; the Players arrive and meet Hamlet.

Claudius and Gertrude welcome two of Hamlet's childhood friends, Rosencrantz and Guildenstern, hoping that they will **'glean'** from Hamlet **'whether aught unknown to us afflicts him'** (2.2.16-7).

Again, as 1.2, the scene is full of clever diplomatic activity, with ambassadors from Norway returned with a good answer from old king, who's given Young Fortinbras money to raise an army to fight another war elsewhere — diverting the problem from Denmark (which will be asked to let Young Fortinbras march through).

Polonius launches into an irritating rhetorical speech leading to issue of Hamlet's apparent madness. Gertrude snaps, 'More matter with less art' (2.2.95). Gertrude thinks it might be love sickness. Polonius suggests plan to find out truth. By setting up Ophelia as 'bait', he and Claudius will spy on Hamlet, watching responses to Ophelia.

As Hamlet enters, apparently engrossed in a book, the court disperses. Polonius attempts leading questions, Hamlet answers obliquely but with a warped grotesque accuracy. He's armed with the ghost's information and so is very alert to the hypocrisy of courtly show, compounded now by betrayal of Ophelia. He identifies Polonius as **'a fishmonger'** (2.2.172) — smelly, possibly obscene innuendo which Polonius misses. Hamlet's irritated baiting of Polonius could be his **'antic disposition'** but it's also indicative of a high stress level. He reminds us throughout the dialogue that Polonius is specifically Ophelia's meddlesome father as well as one of **'these tedious old fools'** who are easy to mock (2.2.212).

Hamlet Suspects Rosencrantz and Guildenstern

Hamlet relaxes temporarily when he meets Rosencrantz and Guildenstern, whom he calls his **'excellent good friends'** (2.2.217) — yet he still maintains the **'antic disposition'** to mask his true feelings. After exchanging rude jokes about their present situation (living in lady Fortune's private parts), Hamlet flips the conversation into potentially dangerous talk about the misfortune of being sent to the **'prison'** of Denmark (2.2.231-40). When they quibble about this description, Hamlet throws away a line that pinpoints a thematic aspect of thought: **'there is nothing either good or bad but thinking makes it so'** (2.2.239-40).

Something makes him suspicious of Rosencrantz and Guildenstern's friendliness. Having extracted their incompetent confession that they *were* sent for, he launches into long speech (2.2.278-92) about his state of mind that is designed to feed them a false impression to report to Claudius. He describes detailed symptoms of *melancholy*, the Elizabethan version of non-specific depression at the apparent meaninglessness of life. Hamlet's speech is often quoted and sounds wonderfully philosophical — the dilemma of a Renaissance mind experiencing its own human transience — but this is a game, not necessarily what Hamlet actually believes or, at most, represents only part of the anguish churning inside him since hearing the ghost's account of murder.

Amicable conversation is re-established when Rosencrantz tells Hamlet about the arrival of a troupe of Players, who have arrived specifically to play for him, partly because they've been forced to travel for work. This leads to an animated exchange on the hot topic of adult tragedians being rivalled by newly fashionable companies of boy actors in 'the city'. (London around 1600 had at least two successful children's companies.) Although the conversation interests him, Hamlet is inevitably preoccupied by the very idea of 'playing' roles in another sense, as his first comment indicates: **'He that plays the king shall be welcome'** (2.2.298). Even news of the public's eagerness to prefer the fad of children over adult actors for serious adult dramas (something theatregoers would usually deride) gives Hamlet reason to reflect on something personal. The very people who mocked Claudius while Old Hamlet was alive now spend big money on fashionable miniature portraits of the new king. It's another sign of a state going wrong. His friendliness to Rosencrantz and Guildenstern evaporates in the savagely witty 'nonsense' of the 'hawk and handsaw' speech (2.2.347-8) to convince them he's mad.

The Arrival of the Players

The Players are preceded onstage by Polonius, long-winded as ever in his description of their repertoire. Hamlet, playing deranged, teases Polonius with a biblical reference about a father and daughter (Jephtha, who was forced by an oath to sacrifice his beloved virgin daughter). Polonius is unsure where the suggestive conversation is heading — fortunately for him, Hamlet turns his attention to the Players as they enter.

Hamlet's conversation with the Players is in prose, excited but apparently sane, unforced and intimate, sounding less like a prince addressing dramatic servants than a dynamic fellow-tragedian greeting friends. Hamlet demonstrates his excellent memory by reciting part of a bloodcurdling speech from a classical drama he's heard the Player speak once before. Note the following two important points:

- Firstly, an Elizabethan audience would recognise that this declamatory style was overblown, a bit old-fashioned but nonetheless very noble, befitting its epic subject, and powerful at engaging the listeners' emotions.

- Secondly, why has Hamlet remembered this particular speech so vividly? It's appropriate to his situation, because it describes the son of Achilles, Pyrrhus, who went to Troy to avenge his father's death. The way Greek Pyrrhus takes his revenge, however, is not characteristic of Renaissance Hamlet's behaviour patterns. The scene described, continued by the Player, is grossly horrific: driven by bloodlust, Pyrrhus slaughters Trojans in the streets, then attacks old King Priam, whose dismemberment is witnessed by his distraught wife, Queen Hecuba.

Key Point

For the moment in performance Hamlet releases his unformed vengeful feelings, using the words of a formally patterned verse drama to experience vicariously how revenge can be enacted. As he listens to the Player recite and sees tears of pity spring into his eyes for Hecuba, Hamlet is driven to think of his own dilemma in relation to the power of theatre to stir deep emotions.

The players leave with Polonius, after their leader has received instructions from Hamlet about a specific play, *The Murder of Gonzago*, that he wants to see performed before the court. He will write a new speech for this.

SOLILOQUY 3: 'O what a rogue and peasant slave am I!' (2.2.502-58) Hamlet's soliloquy is high rhetoric, too — but very different from the Pyrrhus speech, sounding like the thoughts of a 'real' person. He speculates about a Player's capacity to act out passions. If a Player can imagine himself feeling sorrow and actually cry, **'in a fiction, in a dream of passion...all for nothing'** (2.2.504-9) what would he do **'had he the motive and the cue for passion'** (2.2.513) that Hamlet knows he actually has? He tries to wind himself up into a rage but can't. Recognising that drama has power to make people react gives him the idea of confirming the ghost's truthfulness through staging a court show. Hamlet still harbours doubts because he knows he's in a susceptible state of mind. If Claudius is guilty of murder his conscience will be touched at a play about murder. Act 2 closes on this upbeat note as, at last, Hamlet feels he can do something towards revenge.

Act 3

Key Scene

3.1 is a key scene of several sections: Rosencrantz and Guildenstern report on Hamlet's mental state; the famous 'To be or not to be' soliloquy; Hamlet challenges Ophelia, Claudius eavesdrops on them and plans to send Hamlet abroad.

Rosencrantz and Guildenstern deliver their report on Hamlet's **'crafty madness'** to Claudius, who knows it's put on but not exactly *why* Hamlet is doing it — how can he have found out about his father's murder? Gertrude trusts Claudius and Polonius, setting up Ophelia so that she can meet Hamlet 'by chance' while they eavesdrop legitimately (that is, for the safety of the state). Polonius expresses slight discomfort to be setting up a hypocritical show, to **'sugar o'er / The devil himself'** (3.1.48-9). For the first time, the audience hears Claudius admit **'How smart a lash that speech doth give my conscience!'** (aside) (3.1.50).

The **'nunnery' scene** begins. At first Hamlet does not see Ophelia loitering nervously nearby: while she only pretends to be engrossed in her holy book, Hamlet is genuinely engrossed in his meditation about suicide, expressed in the form of another soliloquy.

SOLILOQUY 4: 'To be or not to be, that is the question...' (3.1.56-88)
This is the most often-quoted of Hamlet's soliloquies. In performance it used to be delivered in a solemn 'theatrical' manner, as though it were the key to the entire play but, at the same time, could be lifted out of context to stand for a kind of universal truism about life and death. Modern actors read the speech as more introspective and personal, illustrating how Hamlet the individual is wrestling with the possibility of

suicide as a way of resolving his deeply conflicted feelings. The ghost's demand for revenge commits him to a course of violent action (another murder), contrary to both his student training in reason and logic and the natural inclination of his sharp human intelligence. So he weighs up an alternative — to kill himself instead. What holds him back? Speculation about what happens after death.

Hamlet Challenges Ophelia

Catching sight of Ophelia, Hamlet is wary because, after breaking off meetings and avoiding him, she now materialises, improbably reading her prayer book, right in his way. Following Polonius's instructions, Ophelia tries to return Hamlet's gifts. Her unconvincing rejection speech strains to express poetic disappointment at her **'unkind'** (3.1.101) lover. Who's being unkind?! Hamlet challenges Ophelia because he's following an obsessive train of thought that began with his mother's immorality and betrayal, now extended to include Ophelia, who appears to have spurned his love for no reason. Ophelia herself is frightened and hurt when he speaks brutally, apparently contradicting himself about loving her once and not loving her at all.

How much is Hamlet in control of his feelings? If at least part of his behaviour is put on, it's a good example of his **'antic disposition'** — playing mad in self-defence. Maybe he's guessed that Ophelia, wandering alone, is a decoy and that someone else is spying on their meeting. Precisely *where* in the scene he could realise this is uncertain — and it's up to the actors to suggest the moment onstage. In performance, Hamlet's question **'Where's your father?'** (3.1.126) may cue Ophelia to give a startled glance around her or hesitate for a fraction of a second before replying. Examine the play text for other possible discovery moments and compare actors' choices in film versions of the scene.

Whatever kind of 'madness' or blend of both genuine and put-on derangement you decide Hamlet is expressing, notice how his attack on Ophelia intensifies after that moment, as he urges her repeatedly to **'escape calumny'** (3.1.132-3) (to avoid defamation for being an immoral woman) by forgetting about marriage and becoming a nun. Elizabethan audiences may well have detected a savage joke in the word **'nunnery'**, contemporary slang for 'brothel', in which case Hamlet is crudely implying that Ophelia might as well become a professional immoral woman immediately, since that's the way all women go. His wild speech, ending with the pointed comments on marriages, may be a parting shot intended primarily for the eavesdroppers and calculated to send out a specific warning to Claudius about *his* soon to be ended corrupt marriage.

Ophelia, at the receiving end but unaware of Hamlet's deeper motivations, fails to understand any meaning beyond that he has no desire to marry *her* and concludes that he's completely insane. Her interjections in Hamlet's onslaught don't add up to much on the page but must be understood in performance to be expressing profound shock and fear, leading to her short but poignant soliloquy on the combination of courtier, soldier and scholar whom she loved and admired.

Key Speech

'Oh what a noble mind is here o'erthrown!...' (3.1.144-55)
Emerging from hiding, Claudius immediately negates Ophelia's assessment of Hamlet as mad. It's neither love nor madness but **'something in his soul / O'er which his melancholy sits on brood'** (3.1.158-9). What he's brooding over will hatch eventually and may be dangerous. Claudius thinks his secret crime is still undetected (he never knows about the ghost) but plans to be rid of Hamlet by pretending to send him abroad for his health. A mission to England to collect 'our neglected tribute' (money called 'the Danegeld' paid by England to stop Viking raids) sounds sensible to Polonius.

Polonius still thinks it all started with **'neglected love'** (3.1.172) and we know he may be right. He suggests that if Gertrude will talk to Hamlet after the play (that is presently being arranged) he will eavesdrop on that conversation to see if he can find out more. Claudius agrees that 'Madness in great ones should not unwatched go' (3.1.182).

Key Scene

3.2 The *Mousetrap* play is performed
Hamlet, quite sane, gives his Players some performance notes. He's knowledgeable about theatre practices and eager to make the Play work. In a **Key Speech,** Hamlet explains how he values Horatio (3.2.46-77).

Hamlet sees Horatio, the **'man / That is not passion's slave'** (3.2.61-2), as a trusted friend, and primes him to be on lookout for Claudius's reaction to the play. Hamlet still worries about verifying the ghost's story — he must be sure it isn't a devil and that he isn't giving way to his imagination. As the court enters, Hamlet indicates that he's going to play mad again, 'be idle' (3.2.80).

Hamlet mocks Polonius, embarrasses Ophelia, and makes a pointed reference to his mother's happiness and his father's death 'within's two hours' (3.2.113). *Note that his mad language is all meaningful.* The Play begins after a Dumb Show, traditional but old-fashioned theatre, where a synopsis of the action to come is shown in a brief mime. The Player King emphasises his thirty-year marriage. Hamlet is thirty, so this parallels his parents' marriage. Every line is intentionally suggestive, for example, **'None wed the second but who killed the first'** (3.2.161).

When Claudius asks about 'offence' in a play about adultery and murder, Hamlet plays the simpleton to protect himself, arguing yes, there's a poisoning in it, but it's only pretend, a play…there's **'no offence i'th'world'** (3.2.214) (the world of the Play, that is, but there *is* offence in the real world of the Danish court). The *Mousetrap* play catches the mouse: Claudius stops the Play and leaves. Hamlet is jubilant: **'I'll take the ghost's word for a thousand pound'** (3.2.260-1).

Rosencrantz and Guildenstern tell Hamlet that his mother is waiting for him. Before leaving, he teases them about playing recorders, ending in a furious outburst **'S'blood, do you think I am easier to be played upon than a pipe?'** (3.2.334). Polonius repeats the request that he go to his mother. Again Hamlet baits Polonius, aware that **'They fool me / to the top of my bent'** (3.2.345-6). Alone onstage, Hamlet considers briefly how he will deal with Gertrude.

SOLILOQUY 5: ''Tis now the very witching time of night…' (3.2.349-60)
After firing himself up to act, with strong words about acting in the **'witching time of night'** (3.2.349) and drinking **'hot blood'** (3.2.351), Hamlet recollects that it is his mother he's going to meet. Unlike Nero (the mad Roman Emperor who murdered his own mother) Hamlet plans to modify his violence to words alone, **'I will speak daggers to her but use none'** (3.2.357).

3.3 Claudius Immediately after the Play

Having reported Hamlet's violent state, Rosencrantz and Guildenstern become implicated in the king's plan to send Hamlet to England. Rosencrantz's speech about the importance of protecting the monarch for the general good sounds fine in itself, but rings hollow when the audience has just seen apparent proof of Claudius's own regicide. Polonius reminds Claudius that, as the king's faithful servant, he'll eavesdrop on the imminent meeting because Hamlet's mother might edit her report to protect her son.

Key Speech

Claudius's Soliloquy (3.3.36-72)

Alone, Claudius attempts to pray, revealing in a confessional soliloquy intense psychological conflict. Having gained the crown and Gertrude through murder, he already knows the answer to his rhetorical question: **'May one be pardoned and retain th'offence?'** (3.3.56). As he kneels in silence, Hamlet, on his way to his mother, passes by and sees Claudius off guard. This is a classic dramatic opportunity for the revenger.

SOLILOQUY 6: 'Now might I do it pat, now a is a-praying...' (3.3.73-96)

Hamlet's first impulse to kill Claudius instantly is diverted by a moment's thought about consequences: **'And so I am revenged. That would be scanned'** (3.3.75). He reasons that if he kills Claudius praying, the king's soul will be in a state of grace and will go to heaven, unlike his own father's soul which, the ghost said, must endure torments because he was murdered in his sleep **'in the blossoms of [his] sin'** (1.5.76). Hamlet wants to make sure that Claudius goes to Hell, by choosing a moment when he's indulging his sins, like drinking, being angry, swearing, or indulging in **'incestuous pleasure'** with Gertrude (3.3.88-95).

Hamlet sheathes his sword and goes off to meet his mother. In a superbly ironic moment Claudius gives up trying to pray, telling the audience that his prayers are worthless because his thoughts are earthbound and **'Words without thoughts never to heaven go'** (3.3.98).

Key Scene

3.4 The 'Closet' Scene A closet was a small private sitting room, but this scene is usually set in Gertrude's bedroom to underline the sexual overtones of the interaction between mother and son (see film versions). In this scene Polonius will be killed while he is spying on Hamlet's crucial conversation with his mother.

Before Hamlet's arrival, Polonius instructs Gertrude to be tough in her approach, then hides behind the arras (tapestry wall-hanging). Note how the queen responds to Polonius's coaching.

The tense situation escalates from the moment Hamlet enters. Gertrude gets straight to the point but her innocent pairing of the words 'father' and 'offended' is unfortunate. In performance, she's alerted by his stress on the word 'my' in **'you have *my* father much offended'** (3.4.10), but isn't prepared to take the argument further after her motherly reprimand about his **'idle tongue'** (cheeky retort) draws an even more aggressive response from him about her **'wicked tongue'**. Her fear that Hamlet is truly deranged seems justified when he drags her to a mirror and forces her to sit down: she may well believe that he's about to murder her.

When Polonius, who is supposed to keep silent, responds to her cry for help, Hamlet plunges his sword through the arras, without pausing to think. Is this the moment of his revenge, he asks: **'is it the king?'** (3.4.26). This is a **Key Moment** because it's his first spontaneous act as a revenger — and it results in killing the wrong man.

Gertrude is stunned both by Hamlet's violent action and his accusation about her own **'bloody deed'**, to **'kill a king and marry with his brother'** (3.4.29). Even if she realises what Hamlet is implying about murder in the family, she is slow to understand why he's accusing her: **'What have I done…?'** (3.4.39)…**'what act?'** (3.4.51). Sexual guilt dawns on her slowly as he compares pictures of Old Hamlet and Claudius, evoking disgusting images of her incestuous marriage bed. Then, in mid-rant, Hamlet is stopped in his tracks by the brief reappearance of the ghost.

This intrusion complicates the interview at a crucial moment because Gertrude can't see anything. When Hamlet begins to speak to **'th'incorporal air'** (3.4.117), she assumes that he's mad after all. He then turns the argument back by sheer force of intellect, challenging her not to excuse her real sexual **'trespass'** (3.4.147) by dismissing what he's said as mad talk — she knows she's guilty. The image he uses of an ulcer, covered over but still festering unseen in her soul, is hideous but intensely motivating to Gertrude (3.4.145-50). Heartbroken, she agrees to Hamlet's plan to let Claudius know he's **'But mad in craft'** (3.4.189), to provoke a further response. Hamlet removes Polonius's corpse with a touch of wry humour about the now **'most still, most secret, and most grave'** counsellor who was such a **'foolish prating knave'** in life (3.4.215-6).

Act 4

4.1 Action follows on; Gertrude tells Claudius that Hamlet killed Polonius

Gertrude, still in shock, tells Claudius how Hamlet **'In his lawless fit'** (4.1.8) has just killed Polonius. Claudius, aware that he is Hamlet's real target, confesses to Gertrude that his **'soul is full of discord and dismay'** (4.1.45), yet swings efficiently into damage control and maintains a regal front to Rosencrantz and Guildenstern, who are sent to find the body.

4.2 Rosencrantz and Guildenstern meet Hamlet but fail to understand him

Hamlet tells Rosencrantz and Guildenstern immediately that he can see through them, insulting Rosencrantz for being so obviously the king's **'sponge'** (4.2.12). They fail to understand his 'mad' witty clue that **'The body is with the king, but the king is not with the body'** (4.2.24). The audience hears only too well Hamlet's grim warning in the line — Polonius's dead body is with the dead king (Old Hamlet), but king Claudius is not with Polonius's body, that is, not yet dead, as he is supposed to be. **'The king is a thing...Of nothing'** (4.2.25-7) continues the word game: Claudius's claim to be king is illegitimate, 'nothing', and the man himself is worthless in Hamlet's eyes. The 'antic disposition' has become a kind of buoyant hysteria in Hamlet that carries him through the next scene.

4.3 Hamlet sent to England

The astute politician, Claudius explains that he must act cautiously to restrain Hamlet because **'He's loved of the distracted multitude'** (4.3.4). Hamlet's 'mad' moralising about everything ending up as supper for worms must strike Claudius personally. Consider how many ways his **'Alas, alas'** (4.3.24) could be interpreted. Pretending to be acting for Hamlet's **'especial safety'** (4.3.37), Claudius hurries him aboard ship, escorted by Rosencrantz and Guildenstern, who carry sealed instructions to the king of England on how to deal with Hamlet.

4.4 Young Fortinbras arrives with his army

Fortinbras is awaiting permission to pass through Denmark, as agreed, en route to invade part of Poland. Look back at **2.2** for background to this diplomatic agreement. Hamlet, on his way to the ship, learns from an army captain that Fortinbras and his troops will attack a heavily garrisoned force on a small, worthless piece of ground. Alone, he speculates on this futile activity and his own lack of motivation to carry revenge into action.

SOLILOQUY 7: 'How all occasions do inform against me...' (4.4.32-66)
Hamlet tortures himself for thinking instead of acting, yet also knows that a capacity for reason is the greatest human gift worth having. Watching the Norwegian army, he faces a terrible paradox. Fortinbras is making war for nothing but honour's sake, that's reason enough. Even though thousands of men will die pointlessly, the army moves on **'for a fantasy and trick of fame'** (4.4.61). Hamlet is both appalled and fascinated by Fortinbras, whom he envies for being so sure of his actions. In his own situation he knows he's a tardy revenger. He's trying to whip himself up into activity by focusing **'from this time forth [on] bloody thoughts'** (4.4.65-6).

Key Scene

4.5 Some days later, Ophelia is mad, Laertes becomes a revenger

Ophelia has gone mad, an accumulation of grief and shock after Hamlet's sexually gross treatment of her and her father's murder. Although she's raving, people listen, trying to make sense of her speech. Horatio, knowing that Hamlet is implicated, shows political astuteness when he prompts Gertrude to see Ophelia, to avert **'Dangerous conjectures in ill-breeding minds'** (4.5.15).

Note the stage direction: 'Enter Ophelia distracted.' Remember that she catalogued Hamlet's symptoms of **'a noble mind...o'erthrown'** (3.1.144+). Consider how her genuine madness is being constructed in this scene, and what obsessions are driving her songs and speeches. She jumbles together references to pilgrims, lonely lovers, people being changed or dead, Hamlet and Polonius, lost virginity and sexual betrayal, ending ominously with **'My / brother shall know of it'** (4.5.69-70). Her plight moves Claudius. Notice how he orders that she be carefully looked after as she drifts out. He realises he's losing the political advantage: Laertes already knows about Polonius's hasty burial, and popular rumours abound.

Q How do you respond to the intimate speech in which Claudius expresses his love for Gertrude and confesses to her the **'battalions'** (4.5.78) of **'sorrows'** (4.5.77) that overwhelm him? Is he speaking honestly to her? Have sorrows entered Denmark like an invading army?

In a sudden change of pace in the scene, Laertes, and the mob who wants him as the new king, break down the doors and confront Claudius. His nerve is admirable but can he (who murdered a king) invoke divine right, truly believing **'There's such divinity doth hedge a king'** (4.5.124) that he is protected by God against treason? Notice how Claudius asserts his majestic dominance simply by shifting into the royal plural, speaking of himself in the king's person as 'we' instead of 'I'. His calmness cools Laertes' fury temporarily but before Claudius can say more, Ophelia returns, **'a document in madness'** (4.5.176).

Laertes' speech about his **'kind sister'** (4.5.158) expresses everyone's anguish that **'a young maid's wits / Should be as mortal as an old man's life'** (4.5.159-60). Her choice of flowers for Laertes, Claudius and Gertrude are all symbolically appropriate: rosemary (remembrance, sprigs given at funerals), pansies (*pensées*, thoughts), fennel (flattery), columbine (ingratitude), rue (repentance), daisy (in Ovid's *Metamorphoses*, symbol of Queen Alcestis, good wife), violet (faithfulness, modesty). Together with her fractured songs, blending lines from bawdy ballads with love laments, the flowers coherently pinpoint betrayal and grief as sources of her breakdown.

After Ophelia's exit, Claudius knows that Laertes will be even more set on vengeance, so calculates his response carefully, balancing what his royal plural 'voice' speaks against a more familiar tone of fellow-feeling with Laertes (4.5.197-207). Laertes refocuses on the unanswered question of correct procedure in his father's death — honour demands satisfaction, since Polonius has been denied the **'formal ostentation'** (4.5.210) (ceremonial show) he deserved. Again in command of the situation, Claudius is hypocritical enough to make the big rhetorical gesture, **'And where th'offence is, let the great axe fall'** (4.5.213). This prediction, we guess, will inevitably rebound on him somehow as the tragedy plays out.

4.6 A sailor gives Horatio a letter from Hamlet

Hamlet is supposedly well on his way to England. Horatio reads how a chance encounter with pirates has given Hamlet the opportunity to return to Denmark alone, with serious news to tell his friend.

4.7 Claudius under Threat

Claudius, having told Laertes that Hamlet killed Polonius and threatens his own life, has to answer Laertes' reasonable question, why he **'proceeded not against these feats, / So crimeful and so capital in nature'** (4.7.6-7). Is there any truth in the two reasons Claudius gives in reply? He says that his love for Gertrude prevents him from proceeding against her beloved son, and also that the common people love Hamlet. There's an advantage to Claudius in stalling for time with Laertes: he thinks that Hamlet is soon going to be executed in England, putting an end to any chance that Hamlet might implicate him in the intrigue which brought about Polonius's death or other, still hidden, crimes. No sooner has he hinted to the still fuming Laertes that vengeful action against Hamlet may already be in hand surreptitiously, **'You shortly shall hear more'** (4.7.33), than a messenger arrives with letters from Hamlet. This must be a profoundly stunning dramatic moment for Claudius, yet notice how he recovers, immediately seeing how Laertes' unsatisfied rage may work to his advantage. Hamlet announces that he will meet Claudius the following day. With great skill, Claudius works quickly. He flatters Laertes for his swordsmanship, hinting that Hamlet envies his skill, then fires him up to desire violent revenge.

Key Speech

Claudius (4.7.110-22) reveals his own view about action and what gets in the way of carrying out plans. The imagery is repulsively vivid and changes quickly: love is like a 'candle' that burns bright at first, then burns dull as the candle melts and the 'wick' is suffocated, and that's like an inflammation, **'plurisy'** (4.7.116), where the breath gets suffocated by too much fluid in the lungs. We should act *when* we first have the impulse and want to — **'when we would'** (4.7.118), argues Claudius, because the desire to act gets blocked by delays and it hurts more in the end. Hamlet is like the painful centre, **'the quick of th'ulcer'** (4.7.122) that has to be dealt with at once.

Laertes and Revenge

Asked what he would **'undertake'** (4.7.123) to prove himself a vengeful son, the now excited Laertes imagines a barbaric revenge scenario **'To cut his throat i'th'church'** (4.7.125). In a smooth rebuke, distinguishing between murder and revenge, Claudius signals his approval of Laertes' bloody impulse, while holding that energy in check until Hamlet's certain death in a duelling contest can be set up. Laertes, he says, will be sure to find a real rapier, not a blunt-ended sporting weapon, hidden amongst the selection of foils offered. While Claudius explains the details he also testifies to Hamlet's guileless personality, **'He being remiss** (not careful)**, / Most generous, and free from all contriving** (lacking suspicion)**, / Will not peruse the foils'** (4.7.133-5). Laertes adds a further touch — he will coat his blade with deadly poison so that even if Hamlet is only scratched he will die. The poison suggestion leads Claudius to another refinement: a poisoned drink for Hamlet. The lengths to which they intend to go to ensure that Hamlet dies push the dialogue towards grotesque farce, but their plot for overkill is interrupted by Gertrude's tragic news of Ophelia, which ends the scene.

Key Speech

In this famous speech (4.7.166-83), Gertrude evokes a sad lyrical picture of a demented girl falling into a stream and passively floating along, singing, until dragged under the water to drown. The dreamlike, distanced quality of Gertrude's description is reminiscent of a Messenger's report of a significant death offstage in classical Greek theatre and it serves a similar dramatic purpose: it provides that horrific momentary pause in the tragic action before the final catastrophe. There's nothing to be done but lament it, know it will compound the terrible outcome, and hold it imaginatively in the 'mind's eye' (a phrase used by both Horatio 1.1.112 and Hamlet 1.2.185).

Act 5

Key Scene

5.1 The 'Graveyard' Scene

Two 'clowns', that is, simple folk — here the gravedigger and his assistant — wrestle with the problematic issue of how to justify a Christian burial for a case of suicide. Although she is not mentioned by name, we infer they are discussing Ophelia as they dig her grave. Their conversation sounds comic because they mangle legal arguments, mispronounce words, show off and vie with each other to explain tricky technical details. What they are discussing, however, is not funny.

This Scene is NOT Comic Relief

Like all Shakespearean comic dialogue in otherwise serious plays, this is NOT 'comic relief', time out from the deadly serious material of the play. Avoid using the term 'comic relief' completely: never critically accurate, it suggests that the reader's or viewer's attention can switch off temporarily and just be entertained by the antics of dimwitted characters until the next serious bit comes along.

Key Point

Comic interactions in Shakespeare always reflect upon serious themes, giving us another perspective on a situation or offering a new way of understanding characters.

The opening dialogue and Hamlet's famous conversation with the gravedigger that follows should be read more as inventive 'gallows humour' (virtuoso wordplay on grim subjects in dire circumstances) than playing for laughs.

Suicide, self-murder, in Shakespeare's time was considered a mortal sin. The body could not be buried according to Christian rites and the soul was considered damned. Hamlet struggles to deal with suicide and its ramifications in Soliloquies 1 and 4. Legally, any attempt at suicide that failed could lead to the unfortunate person being prosecuted and punished — the statute was modified in English law only in the twentieth century.

Nowadays the coroner's verdict on Ophelia would probably be

that her death was accidental, caused 'while the balance of her mind was disturbed'. In terms of what emotional distress she has suffered at the hands of Polonius and Hamlet, the gravedigger may have hit on a plausible explanation for Ophelia's terminal breakdown (self-defence) in his retort to his assistant's confirmation that she's to have Christian burial: **'How can that be, unless she drowned herself in her own defence?'** (5.1.5). In any case, he agrees with his workmate that the coroner's decision is still open to question. The class-criticism is telling: **'If this had not been a gentlewoman, she should have been buried out o'Christian burial...Why, there thou sayst'** (5.1.20-3).

After another exchange of wit about what it means to be a gravedigger, which prepares the audience for Hamlet's meditations about death and change in the next part of the scene, the assistant is sent off to buy **liquor**. Hamlet and Horatio enter as the gravedigger breaks into song. Although Hamlet finds it shocking that he can be so cheerful, Horatio's wise comment that **'Custom hath made it in him a property of easiness'** (5.1.57) leads Hamlet to a significant realisation about how easily someone in a privileged state can be repelled by unpleasant realities. Wry self-criticism is discernible in his good-humoured response to Horatio: **''Tis e'en so, the hand of little employment hath the daintier sense'** (5.1.58-9).

Speculating about a skull tossed out of the new grave, Hamlet makes pointed jokes about people who consider themselves important in life — politicians, courtiers, lawyers, ladies — all finally reduced to bits of bone to be thrown about. Any audience, rubbing shoulders at the Globe then, or in the newest theatre now, hears the same grim message about inevitable loss of beauty and dignity in death. Hamlet's philosophical moment unites everyone in the theatre in the bond of common humanity. Hamlet is intrigued by the gravedigger's gossip about himself. While the joke about Hamlet's craziness being unnoticed by the mad English makes audiences smile, the gravedigger can't say how or why Hamlet is mad, it's just common knowledge that he is and that he's been sent away.

We find out now that Hamlet is thirty years old, a mature man, not, as he is often imagined and played, a youthful student. He has spent years becoming the highly educated philosopher prince, but for what purpose? The gravedigger's conversation reconnects Hamlet with his own history, stimulating in him a poignant awareness of how quickly life passes and the body crumbles to dust. Hamlet tries to understand how he can be revolted by Yorick's skull, seeing that no trace remains of the affectionate witty personality, the court jester, he knew and loved as a child. His thoughts in this scene reach as far as they possibly can into that mixture of horrified curiosity people experience when confronting the idea of their own mortality. Horatio, probably alerted to Hamlet's rising agitation at the end of the Yorick speech (when his thoughts turn to a woman's transient and deceptive beauty) gently warns him that it would be carrying thinking too far, **'to consider too curiously'** (5.1.174), to worry that even world heroes like Alexander the Great and Julius Caesar end up as dust. Hamlet can't know that the approaching funeral is Ophelia's but he notices instantly the inappropriateness of **'such maimèd rites'** (5.1.186). He hears the priest's hard response, before Laertes' outburst: **'A ministering angel shall my sister be'** (5.1.208) reveals the body's identity.

Gertrude's loving farewell to Ophelia **'I hoped thou shouldst have been my Hamlet's wife'** (5.1.211) suggests that she knew of Hamlet's interest in Ophelia and, unlike Polonius, saw no problem in it. Moments later, Laertes jumps into Ophelia's grave in an extravagant show of grief, then Hamlet rushes out of hiding to claim **'I loved Ophelia'** (5.1.236). In performance, both men may leap into the grave and fight there. Alternatively, Laertes the revenger leaps out when he hears Hamlet accuse him of 'ranting'. Significantly, Hamlet responds with shock when attacked by Laertes. **'What is the reason that you use me thus? / I loved you ever'** (5.1.256-7). Has he forgotten that he killed Polonius? As Hamlet is escorted away, Claudius tells Laertes that the duel must be set up immediately.

Key Scene

5.2 The duel: Hamlet enacts his revenge

Hamlet describes to Horatio how, on board ship, he managed to read the letter Rosencrantz and Guildenstern were carrying from Claudius to England, containing instructions for his execution. He wrote and sealed a substitute letter, condemning them to instant death **'Not shriving time allowed'** (5.2.47), so that they wouldn't have time to talk — but also denying them time to pray, just like Claudius killed Old Hamlet. In

Hamlet's view, this was all made possible by divine will. Horatio agrees when told **'There's a divinity that shapes our ends, / Rough-hew them how we will'** (5.2.10-11). Having his father's royal seal with him made it possible for Hamlet to create plausible substitute letters, leading him to assert that **'even in that was heaven ordinant'** (5.2.48).

Responding to Horatio's misgivings about his brutality to Rosencrantz and Guildenstern, he asserts they have only themselves to blame for their own **'insinuation'** (5.2.59) into a superior duel between himself and Claudius, **'the pass and fell incensèd points / Of mighty opposites'** (5.2.61-2). Considering what Laertes is planning with Claudius the metaphor is ironically apt — we know that the sham duel will certainly be played out with 'incensèd points', not as a battle between 'mighty opposites' but as a staged execution. Hamlet's ignorance of their plotting makes his next generous speech about befriending Laertes **'For by the image of my cause, I see / The portraiture of his'** (5.2.77-8) equally ironic.

A foppish young courtier called Osric appears, bearing the formal invitation to the show duel on which, he says, Claudius has wagered valuable horses and weapons. Hamlet enjoys befuddling the over-polite fool with an exaggerated form of his own flowery court language, before agreeing to take up the challenge and win for the king.

Alone with Horatio, Hamlet admits to a premonition, **'how ill all's here about my heart'** (5.2.186), prompting his friend to urge **'If your mind dislike anything, obey it'** (5.2.190). In a **Key Speech** (5.2.192-6), Hamlet accepts, even if the duel will bring about his death, the fundamental truth that **'the readiness is all'** (5.2.194-5).

The court assembles. Is Hamlet being sincere when he asks Laertes' forgiveness, blaming his **'sore distraction'** (genuine madness) (5.2.202) for the damage he has done? How could this affect Laertes' plan for revenge? Hamlet has diffused some of his immediate passion for revenge but he insists that the question of family 'honour' demands satisfaction, to be settled in the supposedly friendly duel.

Notice how Laertes fusses to make sure he gets the correct rapier as planned (5.2.236) and how Claudius makes a big public show of dropping what looks like a rich pearl into Hamlet's cup when he goes into the lead with the first hit. In Elizabethan times it would be recognised as an extravagantly generous gesture, acknowledging the worth of both the donor and the drinker, to dissolve precious pearls in wine. Cleopatra does it at a feast for her lover Antony in a later Shakespeare play. Here the theatrical sham of giving masks deadly betrayal — the drink becomes 'precious' only because it contains the backup poison for Hamlet, who cannot be induced to take it. Instead Gertrude picks up the cup to toast her son when Hamlet scores his second hit. Does she guess something may be wrong when Claudius warns her so strongly not to drink?

As the duel gets under way, we are drawn back to the mood of the Play's opening scenes. At Claudius's command (5.2.246-50) there is to be the same noisy carousing with drums, trumpets and cannons that marked the corrupt king's earlier feast, while Hamlet and his friends waited outside in the cold for a ghost. Although the ghost will not appear to witness the last scene of vengeance, it has been called ominously to mind. Something is rotten in the state of Denmark, but we anticipate it is about to be set right by Hamlet taking his long-delayed revenge.

It happens almost by chance. Claudius loses all control the moment Gertrude falls, contradicting his clumsy lie with her last breath. Hamlet thinks he's in a fair fight until, wounded by Laertes and bleeding, he realises the duel is rigged. With his mother poisoned and Laertes confessing the deadly plot against him, Hamlet at last finds the **'motive and the cue for passion'** (Soliloquy 3, 2.2.513) to complete his act of revenge. He finally articulates his uncle's crimes, **'thou incestuous, murderous, damnèd Dane'** (5.2.304), avenging at once his father's, mother's and his own murder with an appropriate combination of poisoned sword and drink.

Freed of the burden he has carried through the play, Hamlet then drains the cup and dies before Horatio's appalled eyes, naming (of all people) Young Fortinbras as his successor. He charges his closest friend to explain the carnage to Fortinbras **'with conquest come from Poland'** (5.2.329) and the English ambassadors.

Key Speech

Horatio's noble lie (5.2.352-64)

Horatio begins with a downright lie about Rosencrantz and Guildenstern, **'He never gave commandment for their death'** (5.2.353). Horatio carries his own burden of knowledge, being, as Hamlet called him, **'one in suffering all that suffers nothing'** (3.2.56): his first act to protect Hamlet's honour by telling what Elizabethans would accept as a 'noble lie' told for a worthy reason. Although Fortinbras is quick to **'embrace [his] fortune'** (5.2.367) and arrogantly lay claim to the throne of Denmark, Horatio checks his relish for another fight by revealing that Hamlet gave his assent before dying. Horatio, too, urges Fortinbras to display the bodies in public and let him tell the full story: **'Even while men's minds are wild, lest more mischance / On plots and errors happen'** (5.2.373-4). His voice of reason prevails, even though Fortinbras insists on **'The soldier's music and the rite of war'** (5.2.378) to accompany Hamlet's body away.

CHARACTERS & RELATIONSHIPS

Build your own files on individual characters, noting as many details as you can and selecting a few key quotations for each one. Below are some of the key ideas to develop. More discussion of character will be found in the next section exploring themes.

My main focus is on **THEMES, ISSUES & VALUES**, where core ideas of a very complicated play are opened up. Keep returning to the **SCENE-BY-SCENE ANALYSIS** as you develop ideas about characters, themes and issues and always add your own notes to mine. Watch several film versions, too, and remember that a student of the play is like Honigmann's description of 'a good audience [that] takes nothing for granted, but feels its way into the story as this unfolds'.

Character Groups

Older men in power
Claudius, Old Hamlet and Polonius (together with Old Fortinbras of Norway who is not seen in the play) represent a generation of dominant male 'leaders' whose authority is in decline. Old Hamlet and Old Fortinbras established their power through force of arms. Claudius works

more politically, using diplomacy to establish his status outside Denmark while relying on Polonius, his chief counsellor, for domestic intelligence.

Young men at court

Hamlet, Rosencrantz and Guildenstern, Horatio, Laertes and Fortinbras with minor characters who, note, may not all be young — Marcellus, Barnardo, Francisco, Osric, Voltimand, Cornelius and Reynaldo — represent different types of younger men hanging around the intriguing court world.

Q How do they find a place for themselves? Are they all in it to serve their own ambitions?

Women at court

Gertrude and Ophelia have little autonomy, identified by their relationship of obedience to men, Gertrude as queen, widow, wife, mother and Ophelia as daughter, sister, beloved (old-fashioned word used deliberately). They participate in key scenes with main male characters and have limited but important 'solo' moments in the dialogue.

Ordinary folk who know about life and death

These are represented by the gravedigger and his clownish mate, and by the troupe of travelling Players. Hamlet interacts significantly with both of these character groups.

Characters

Hamlet

The Prince of Denmark dominates the play's thematic explorations as well as the very stage or screen in performance. Out of the play's twenty scenes, he is physically present in thirteen, and a topic of conversation in the rest. His questions about everything drive the tragic action. While his inner turmoil is revealed through soliloquies, our awareness of a fuller spectrum in Hamlet's personality develops as we watch his interactions with other characters. With male friends and members of the servant class (gravediggers and Players) he can be versatile, charming and playful but his character is dangerously clever. His relationships with his mother and Ophelia are more difficult to understand. More than shame for his widowed mother's sensuality is speaking when he makes the generalisation 'frailty, thy name is woman' (1.2.146). There are several possible reasons why Hamlet's personality is so edgy and volatile:

- understandable grief for his father's death and mother's remarriage to an uncle he despises

- emotional pain, after seeing the ghost, at his father's ongoing suffering

- the strain of having to attempt to be a revenger when everything in him is repelled by that ethic

- the sudden, inexplicable coolness of the woman he thought was returning his genuine and courtly expression of love, just at the time when he needs to redirect emotional attachment from his mother to a partner.

Q See if you can add further explanations for Hamlet's stress and emotional volatility.

Hamlet and Old Hamlet

Hamlet has a respectful, admiring view of his father, for whom he is grieving as the play begins: we can hear the sad pride in his words to Horatio, 'A was a man, take him for all in all / I shall not look upon his like again' (1.2.187-8). What Hamlet sees in the ghost is the antithesis of a powerful living man, a terrible apparition of a dead father, now a tormented soul in purgatory. Addressing the fully armoured ghost as 'Hamlet, King, father, royal Dane', we can hear Hamlet struggling to restore potency and respect to his father, whose nobility has been further sullied by Gertrude's adultery with Claudius.

Q Do we get the feeling that he loved his father?

Old Hamlet's appearance gives Hamlet the reason he's looking for to turn feelings of disgusted antagonism into action. It's so important for Hamlet to verify the ghost's story, since he's alone when Old Hamlet speaks (1.5.9-91).

Q Could it be that in the emotional crisis after the play (which re-enacted Old Hamlet's murder) he only imagines the ghost's return in 3.4?

Hamlet and Claudius

Hamlet's violent dislike of Claudius stems from the new marriage, rather than being passed over as king, since the Danish monarchy is shown to be elected, not hereditary. He sees through Claudius's show of paternal friendliness in 1.2 and rejects it. He focuses his contempt for his uncle by making negative character comparisons with Old Hamlet, the idealised father.

Q Should we believe his biased views?

Claudius treats Hamlet cautiously when he registers hostility. Having a guilty secret to hide, he accepts some responsibility for setting off Hamlet's disturbance — but never knows that Hamlet has been told by a ghost.

Q Is Claudius reading Hamlet's character well when he tells Laertes that Hamlet will be easy to fool into accepting the final duel because his character is 'remiss (incautious) / Most generous, and free from all contriving' (4.7.133-4)?

Hamlet and Gertrude

The close emotional bond between mother and son is never lost in the play, but Gertrude's remarriage motivates Hamlet's mixed feelings towards her. His imagination supplies disturbingly excessive details of her sex life (3.4) that would sound more appropriate coming from the lips of a jealous lover than a righteously indignant son.

Q Does he ever manage to forgive Gertrude for her adultery and incest?

Q Why is Hamlet obsessed with his mother's sexuality?

Gertrude's speeches support the usual reading of her character in performance as a warm, sensual, mature woman, who is ignorant of Claudius's crimes until Hamlet suggests them in 3.4.

Q Does she reject Claudius after this? Can she be loyal to husband *and* son in the last scene? (See notes on **Love and Sexuality** theme pp.54-61 for relationship analysis.)

Ophelia

It's easy to 'lose' Ophelia, relegating her to the stock type of compliant young woman with no internal interest and no courage. In performance she can seem vapid but beautiful. Is that what makes her interesting to Hamlet? It's sadly ironic that the character who articulates Hamlet's perhaps put-on 'madness' so poignantly and perceptively ('O what a noble mind...' 3.1) should break down into genuine madness herself and die pitifully. (See discussion of the theme of **Madness and 'antic disposition'** pp.61-63 for Ophelia as a 'a document in madness'.)

Ophelia and Hamlet

See notes on **Love and Sexuality** theme for full relationship analysis (pp.54-61).

Claudius

Despite being revealed to be a murderer and political schemer, Claudius first appears as a competent and accepted new ruler of Denmark (1.2). The only descriptions of Claudius, Hamlet's comparison of him with the royal brother he murdered, are disparaging. He's the goat-legged animal 'satyr' to Old Hamlet's sun-god 'Hyperion' in Hamlet's memory, 'no more like my father / Than I to Hercules' (1.2.152-3). Hamlet also calls him 'a mildewed ear' (3.4.64) of corn that infects the crop, a wasteland 'moor' (3.4.67) compared with the 'fair mountain' (3.4.66), his brother (3.4). The soliloquy (3.3.36-72) is the key to human weakness in the revenge-play villain. Claudius feels cursed, identifying himself with Cain, the first biblical murderer of his brother Abel. Led to commit regicide (king murder) and fratricide (brother murder), he cannot relinquish what he has, even to clear his conscience. His 'vicious mole of nature', the tragic flaw that drives him to crime and leads to his death, is a mixture of ambition and desire.

Q Is Claudius as awful as Hamlet paints him?

Claudius and Gertrude

Claudius loves Gertrude enough to have committed murder for her. The ghost suggests that the couple were having an affair while Gertrude was married to Old Hamlet and, by terrible chance, Claudius is responsible for Gertrude's death (his poisoned drink idea).

Q How do you react to Claudius's description of 'our sometime sister, now our queen' (1.2.8)? Do you regard their marriage as incestuous? (See notes on the **Love and Sexuality** theme, pp.54-61, for relationship analysis.)

Gertrude

What does Gertrude know about her present husband's crimes? Nothing, it seems. She appears unconcerned by the content of the *Mousetrap* play and only feels guilt for her adulterous behaviour when Hamlet forces her to bring it to consciousness (3.4).

Her **'vicious mole of nature'** is probably lustful sensuality (according to Hamlet) but this quality has to be brought out in the characterisation onstage, since her speeches on the page more often express loving concern than lechery.

Polonius

Polonius owes something to several figures likely to be known by an Elizabethan audience. Elizabeth's indispensable, powerful but recently dead chief minister, the aristocratic Lord Burghley, was replaced in 1598 by a new kind of career civil servant, the clever, secretive Robert Cecil. Cecil was disliked by courtiers for his Machiavellian way of always knowing what was going on around the Queen. Like Machiavelli, the Italian Prince's shrewd adviser, his business was to protect Elizabeth's interests by any means. As a Machiavellian minister, Polonius, unfortunately, is completely incompetent.

Although Shakespeare uses his own pedantry to mock him and cause laughter, Polonius is not comic. He's an overbearing father, spying on his son and compromising his daughter, another father who is the object of Hamlet's contempt and his comic butt.

Q Does he deserve his death for eavesdropping? You could argue that his **'vicious mole of nature'** is the urge to spy and know secrets.

Horatio

Horatio exists less as a character with his own psychological depth than to be Hamlet's trusted friend. He's sensitive to Hamlet's cynical jokes and moderates Hamlet's rising hysteria in the 'graveyard' scene (5.1), living on to tell Hamlet's story. Hamlet's **Key Speech** (3.2.46-77) denotes Horatio's character, the quiet, accurate observer needed for the *Mousetrap* play.

Laertes

As a young gentleman, Laertes travels the world and feels free to lecture his sister about her virtue. In 4.5 he is a characteristically *heroic* young revenger, acting from emotion, physically on the attack, fearlessly demanding answers about his father's death. Ophelia's death compounds his desire for revenge that Claudius manipulates. Hamlet understands Laertes: 'For by the image of my cause I see, / The portraiture of his' (5.2.77-8).

Fortinbras

A one-dimensional military character, 'strong-armed' as his name indicates. Fortinbras represents an older-style action hero, valuing fine abstractions like Honour and Nobility.

Throughout the play, while Hamlet is battling in the mind, Fortinbras is waging physical wars somewhere else. There's a shade of irony in the way he gets the Danish crown handed to him without having to fight for it.

Rosencrantz and Guildenstern

How does Shakespeare make dramatic use of these indistinguishable time-serving minor courtiers?

Osric

A minor young courtier, usually played 'excessively' as a nervous fop.

What is his purpose? He presents to Hamlet, in the last scene of his life, the extreme foolishness an intelligent person might have to suffer in a royal court. Osric is privileged and fashionable but irritatingly superficial: Hamlet tells Horatio that Osric is just one of a type of fool 'the drossy age dotes on' (5.2.165-70). He has a minor but significant moment in the duel as referee and when he draws attention to Gertrude's dying swoon (5.2.283).

The Players

A group of professional actors Hamlet clearly knows well. They are not individuals, although their leader, known as the First Player, demonstrates his skill as a performer of classic quality in 2.2. Which role would he play in the *Mousetrap* play, the King or the villain? (See **Theatre and Life,** pp.65-6, for more discussion about the significance of the Players.)

The Gravedigger

Turn back to the discussion of 5.1 in the **SCENE-BY-SCENE ANALYSIS** for detailed notes on the gravedigger's conversation with Hamlet. Digging graves for thirty years has given him plenty of life experience and an unsentimental wisdom about processes of decay, even when he's tossing around the skull of Yorick, an old drinking mate 'a whoreson mad fellow...a mad rogue' (5.1.149,151). (See **The Realities of Life and Death**, pp.67-8, for more ideas about the significance of the gravedigger in this play.)

THEMES, ISSUES & VALUES

Hamlet is a complex play, rich in themes and issues. One of its central themes, 'the nature of Revenge', gives rise to many issues related to the legal, psychological, moral and spiritual problems of revenge killing. Many of these relate specifically to the central character, Hamlet. How can he be sure he's justified in killing Claudius? Should he believe a ghost, even if it's his father? How does he compare with other murderers and revengers in the play? Given that Claudius is a murderer, does that give Hamlet further justification? What alternative does he have? What complicates Hamlet's thinking and raises issues for him?

To help you explore such questions (discussion groups are excellent) and to develop your own viewpoint, it is helpful to ponder these questions in a more personal way: 'Do *I* think Hamlet is justified to go for revenge or not? What might I do? What is right or wrong behaviour, anyway? Is it just what's legal, or are there other considerations besides whether you can be punished or not? Is revenge-killing the same as cold-blooded murder, and no more argument about it?

Issues inevitably relate to values. Values in *Hamlet* are those aspects of a particular dramatic scene, or of a character's decisions and choices, that you can pick up to discuss. What is right or wrong behaviour? What personality traits seem to be most valued in a good person? How precious is life? Is honesty as valuable as courage? What happens after death? One of your tasks is to analyse what *Hamlet* brings to bear on such large and important matters.

Every society reinforces its own approved **ideology**, through political, religious and legislative structures. Generally, people within a society agree to abide by a learnt 'consensus opinion' about ethical and moral issues and just tend to do 'the right thing', but this can be a fragile agreement at best, especially in stressful times. As literature students we all need to remind ourselves that plays and films, like other cultural documents, carry their own **ideological messages**. They present a point of view, in a story form that either aims to persuade us overwhelmingly or challenges us to think out things for ourselves.

The following notes give you some introductory material to help you think about the big themes and issues and develop your own viewpoints. However, always remember that when you write on themes, issues and values, your focus is on the text. The broad questions are:

- What do I learn from Shakespeare's *Hamlet* about particular themes, for example, the nature of revenge, or love, or the impact of thought on the ability to act, or guilt?

- How is a specific theme or issue developed in the play?

- What specific *values* are shown to be important in *Hamlet*?

- What is my viewpoint on the important themes, issues and values that help to inform my interpretation of these in *Hamlet*?

The Nature of Revenge

Revenge is all about getting even with someone who has done you wrong by repaying them in kind. You then become the revenger, avenging wrongs done. What they've done to you and yours, you do back to them and theirs. Put as simply as this, revenge may seem a natural impulse and justifiable because it has a kind of poetic justice about it: there's a retributive balancing out of pain and suffering. This punitive view has ancient precedents in many cultures: in the Christian Bible, for instance, you can read the formula expressed as the word of God, 'Vengeance is mine; I will repay, saith the Lord' (Romans 12.19) and 'eye for eye, tooth for tooth, hand for hand, foot for foot' (Exodus 21.24). As many students of *Hamlet* will recognise, this attitude still continues today. You might consider the approach to terrorists and their actions, including the responses to the Bali bombers.

Alternatives to the 'eye-for-eye' revenge model exist. Every day, Australian courts award monetary damages to represent as much as possible an equivalent 'value' to property that has been deliberately destroyed, stolen or lost, or as compensation for personal injury. Wrongdoing may come to light after many years, resulting in prosecution long after victims have given up hope of justice. The New Testament in the Christian Bible records Jesus's even more radical injunction to substitute forgiveness for revenge of any kind, 'Blessed are the peacemakers' (Matthew 5.8) and 'Love your enemies' (Matthew 5.44).

The classic revenge plot, on the stage or in the movies, ends in a scene of wholesale slaughter. Even though it usually leads to death for the original victim, honour is satisfied in the final successful payback. So the idea of 'revenge', across many cultures and in different historical periods, is closely linked to another idea about lost 'honour'. This must be retrieved somehow and can never be satisfied by damage settlements, nor by forgiveness.

Look back at the opening notes on Revenge Tragedy in **Genre** (pp.11-14) and remember what Francis Bacon wrote in 1597. He described revenge as 'a kind of wild justice'. The key word is 'wild', because the lone revenger cannot appeal to law but must take it on himself (or, less often, herself) to carry through the revenge. While it is 'justice', it is not legally sanctioned, often because (as Bacon points out) 'there is no law to remedy' the situation.

Think about the evidence for crime in Hamlet's case. It's a ghost's word against the popular ruler, isn't it? Bacon raises two more complicating factors in the avenging psychology. Firstly, that if a man does take revenge he is getting even with his enemy. It 'solves' the immediate problem. The second point is that if the revenger doesn't act and overlooks the matter, then 'he is superior; for it is a prince's part to pardon'. In other words, the would-be revenger is operating at a higher, moral level, because he is being magnanimous (noble in feeling and conduct - -a great soul), he forgives the crimes and acts in a 'princely' way. In the Renaissance, magnanimity was considered to be one of the great virtues of a leader. Furthermore, warns Bacon, if the revenger remains preoccupied with the idea of revenge, then he 'keeps his own wounds green, which otherwise would heal and do well'. A green wound is one that stays fresh and open, an excellent metaphor for the continued anger and other negative feelings that stay alive in the revenger's mind. This is a key issue for Hamlet, specifically, as he attempts to think through his situation.

Issues to Develop

- What are 'unforgivable' crimes (for example, murder of a sibling or ruler, suicide, treachery)?
- What are 'unpunishable' crimes (for example, ingratitude, abuse, callousness)?
- What are emotional and psychological effects of pursuing vengeance (for example, confusion about values, shock, madness, sexual distress, guilt feelings, despair, sense of dishonour, loss of trust)?
- Is forgiveness a viable alternative to revenge for Hamlet or Laertes?
- What is the connection between revenge and honour for Hamlet, Laertes, and Fortinbras?
- Why is the revenge ethic an *inadequate* motivator for Hamlet?
- Think about Laertes and Fortinbras as two more revengers. Do they achieve their aims?

The issue of **'violence as ongoing warfare'** can be developed as an extension of this overall theme, connecting it with several others. Futile, ongoing warfare drives the world of the play from 1.1, saturating the text with sounds and imagery of weapons, injuries, military tactics and violence.

- Compile a list of these, including Claudius's anguished 'When sorrows come, they come not single spies, / But in battalions' (4.5.77-8).
- Is it intentionally ironic, do you think, and a final critique of the revenge ethic, that Old Hamlet beat Old Fortinbras in a fight before the play began, and Young Fortinbras marches in to claim the Danish throne over Young Hamlet's dead body?

Interplay between Guilt and Responsibility

If, inadvertently, I were to cause harm to someone and find out later, it might lead me to accept at least a degree of responsibility for their pain and suffering. Even if nobody else knew about my part in what had happened, I'd probably feel morally and ethically bound to acknowledge it. I might not feel 'guilty' about it, because the harm I caused was accidental: nonetheless, I'd want to apologise and try to help make amends. Hypothetically, this is how the majority of people might feel in the same situation — responsible but not guilty.

If I chose to do wrong or cause harm deliberately, without witnesses to tell on me, and then decided to conceal my responsibility, I might put on an innocent face and appear calm, even enjoying the benefits of my crime. I might escape retribution as long as my involvement remained secret and if I remained untroubled by conscience. If I didn't care about the moral and ethical consequences of what I'd done, then conscience would be irrelevant — I'd never feel guilt. Two things might happen to challenge my sense of security. Someone or something could be disclosed that would implicate me. Or I could incriminate myself as guilt started to undermine my calm exterior. Internal feelings of guilt come from self-awareness and conscience. I could start to recognise my responsibility for contributing to something wrong. Then I'd have to decide whether to confess or work even harder to repress guilt, maybe committing more crimes to protect myself. More crimes, more responsibility, more guilt, more anguish — a vicious circle, if I had a conscience and was not completely bad.

Now put yourself in the classic 'Revenge scenario'. Someone who plans to commit murder deliberately breaks a fundamental and almost universal societal taboo. That person might be labelled evil or psychotic but the 'revenge ethic' condones murder in certain circumstances. The revenger is encouraged to feel responsible but not guilty for punishing a wrongdoer who cannot be brought to law. In Hamlet's case, the ghost's supernatural command adds horrifying weight to his already conflicted sense of responsibility to his dead father and 'shameful' mother. Hamlet's natural propensity is to be playful, a kind lover to Ophelia, an engaging thinker with his friends, someone who enjoys theatre and thinking. This personality must be jettisoned if he is to play the role of revenger.

Characters who are not entirely bad experience the terrible weight of guilty consciences, notably Claudius (in his confession with the failed prayer, 3.3), and Gertrude, breaking down with horror at the 'black and grainèd spots' in her soul (3.4.89).

Issues to Develop

- Where do Hamlet, the ghost, Claudius, Gertrude, Ophelia, Polonius, Laertes, Rosencrantz and Guildenstern fit on a sliding scale of guilt and/ or responsibility for the damage they inflict on each other in this play?

- Do you think that the ghost (Old Hamlet) is justified in demanding that Hamlet take responsibility for avenging his death?

- Do you think that Claudius exemplifies a man with a genuine conscience?

- Do you think that Gertrude accepts Hamlet's version of events and, feeling guilty and ashamed, knowingly carries through 'justice' on herself at the end?

- How do the Players help to focus issues of guilt and responsibility in their scenes?

Love and Sexuality

Expressing love for someone may or may not involve sex. Also, sexuality means more than just 'having sex', because the word describes an individual's inner awareness of himself or herself as somebody who has a certain biological and social identity, with individual desires and sexual preferences.

In Shakespeare's time, inappropriate or socially disapproved of sexual relationships were dealt with in two main ways. Firstly, through the legal system and secondly, much more effectively, through unofficial social 'policing' that led most people to respect certain rules of conduct, especially about sexual behaviour of women. Men had more freedom, with the single exception of overt homosexual behaviour, although close friendships (sexual or not) seem to have been commonplace. Generalising makes the picture look simpler than it was.

Respectable women were supposed to be virgins until they married, then become wives, mothers and widows. Unattached women who were sexually active were called whores. Many brides went to their official church weddings already pregnant, since sexual relations were usual after friends had witnessed a public betrothal. Rude jokes about widows and sex abounded. They were supposed to stay 'chaste' but many remarried respectably, including several examples among Shakespeare's actor friends, as a matter of economic necessity as well as for love. The play examines this theme in several ways.

Gertrude's Relationships with Old Hamlet and Claudius

Gertrude's relationships with her first and her second husbands are largely seen through Hamlet's eyes. Old Hamlet appears as the idealised first husband and Claudius as the incestuous adulterate beast second husband. The ghost, naturally, stresses his dignified love, compared with brother Claudius, 'whose natural gifts were poor / To those of mine' (1.5.51-2).

Hamlet has a courtly memory of his father like a sun-god 'Hyperion… so loving to my mother / That he might not beteem the winds of heaven / Visit her face too roughly…she would hang on him / As if increase of appetite had grown / By what it fed on…' (1.2.140-5). The ghost accuses his 'most seeming virtuous queen' of adultery (1.5.46).

In Elizabethan England, the Church of England forbade marriage to a brother's wife. (This still stands today.) Claudius tries to excuse the speedy remarriage, admitting that, although the memory of his 'dear brother' is still 'green', affairs of state demanded that Denmark should get back to normal quickly and everyone showed their agreement at the time (1.2). Claudius and Gertrude speak to each other lovingly. She is 'my dear Gertrude' to him in 2.2, an intimate moment in which she speaks frankly about 'our o'erhasty marriage'. In 3.1 he calls her 'sweet Gertrude'. He also reveals his disgust at his own hypocrisy when he applies a metaphor of a painted prostitute (3.1.51-3) to his own situation but not to Gertrude's — she's unaware that he's protecting her from the terrible knowledge that he's committed murder to marry her.

Gertrude cannot interpret Claudius's reaction to the *Mousetrap* play. She accuses Hamlet only of offending his new 'father' by offering obviously tactless subject matter as an entertainment (3.4.9). Annoyed by Hamlet's disapproval of her remarriage, Gertrude responds as an exasperated mother 'Nay, then I'll set those to you that can speak' (3.4.17), only to be told bluntly about her first husband's murder. Gertrude cannot accept Hamlet's murder story completely because she can't see the ghost.

Nonetheless, she accepts Hamlet's criticism of her lecherous guilt as fair. Even after this scene, Gertrude and Claudius comfort and try to protect each other (see 4.1, 4.5, 4.7, 5.2). If you judge their relationship only through Hamlet's disgusted eyes, you miss the subtlety of their adult love, where guilt can prompt pity as well as blame.

Q Is Hamlet justified in attacking his mother for still having sexual desires?

The Fractured Hamlet-Ophelia Relationship

This is a heartbreakingly naive and therefore vulnerable relationship and one I don't think has yet become sexual. Hamlet has sent poetic love letters and made 'private time' to see her and Ophelia accepts that he's being honourable in his holy vows of love. Seen this way, both Laertes' know-all worldly advice to his sister in 1.3 sounds callous but Polonius's follow-up, reducing Hamlet's interest to crude seduction, is even more brutal. They might be mouthing conventional male warnings to young women, familiar to Elizabethan ears, but Ophelia could be less intimidated than it might appear from the words on the page. Look at several film versions for more ideas about playing Ophelia as innocent but not necessarily weak or stupid just because she's a modest virgin.

Laertes may be prudent to warn Ophelia that Hamlet, as a prince, can't 'Carve for himself' (1.3.20), that is, choose a wife according to his appetite, an interesting metaphor. Yet Gertrude obviously assumed there would be no objection to Ophelia as her future daughter-in-law (5.1.211-3). Ophelia *has* to play the obedient Elizabethan daughter: she agrees to return Hamlet's gifts and stop meeting him. The consequences are soon apparent when she reports Hamlet's changed behaviour (2.1.75-98). When he next meets Polonius (2.2), Hamlet may be playing mad but he's also conveying to us the bitterness of frustration in the 'fishmonger, daughter, conception' conversation (see 2.2.170+).

Hamlet releases his emotional anguish in 3.1, the 'nunnery' scene. Set up as bait by her father (who caused the breakdown of trust between the lovers in the first place), Ophelia starts at a disadvantage. As soon as she tells Hamlet she *wants* to return his gifts, although her reluctance should be clear to us in the artificial speech she mouths, his tone changes to cynicism and attack. The 'nunnery' suggestion (with its likely *double-entendre* of brothel) must be offensive and shocking to her. He swerves from personal to general criticism of women, leaving her shocked but convinced he's mad.

The play demonstrates how love turned sour through frustration and disappointment loses its capacity for kindness and turns instead to cynicism and bawdiness — sex becomes nothing more than a dirty joke. Hamlet embarrasses Ophelia in public when he suggests lying 'in her lap' in the 'Play' scene and then pretends to be shocked that *she* might have interpreted his suggestion crudely (3.2.99-107). Soon afterwards, Ophelia loses her inhibitions when she loses her wits — her bawdy songs jar the audience into pity for her wrecked innocent personality (4.4).

The final terrible moment for these unfortunate lovers comes in the 'graveyard' scene (5.1), when Hamlet realises that the body they're burying is hers. His undignified scuffle with Laertes to 'prove' he loved her more than 'forty thousand brothers' (5.1.236) is heartbreaking, a mark of Hamlet's absolute desperation.

Q Is Polonius at all justified in his seedy assumptions about Hamlet as a young man just wanting to seduce Ophelia?

The Ambiguous Mother-Son Relationship

It would be odd if Hamlet, the thinking man, didn't experience powerful, even if unconscious, reasons to delay slaughtering a man he hated. Conflicting love and hatred for his mother would be understandable, too.

Shakespeare gives us a strong sense of Hamlet's hysterical disgust at the thought of his mother in bed with Claudius (See 3.4.91-3, 183-6). Hamlet's ambiguously expressed love for his mother is commonly identified as an Oedipal relationship (developed below).

When Olivier's film version came out in 1948 it was publicised with the tag, 'The tragedy of a man who could not make up his mind'. This description was used to promote the idea that Hamlet was unable to carry out his revenge on Claudius because he was identifying too closely with Claudius — the man who had managed to kill Hamlet's father and marry his mother.

Freud had speculated in 1900 that Hamlet's irresolution might be explained psychologically as an 'Oedipus complex', a term in the new science of the mind derived from the classical Greek story of a hero who accidentally killed his father and married his mother, fulfilling a prophesy that had been made at his birth. In Freud's metaphorical reading it denoted a male's desire, formed in early childhood, but then deeply repressed as taboo and so 'forgotten' by the conscious mind, to get rid of his rival/ father (commit patricide) and keep his mother's affection to himself (commit incest). Hamlet's attitude towards his uncle-father is problematic because Claudius has managed to carry out both of Hamlet's unrecognised desires, argued Freud. Deep down, to kill Claudius would be like killing himself.

In his 1948 film, Laurence Olivier decided to explore a psychoanalytical reading of Hamlet's personality, building his *mise-en-scène* to suggest that Elsinore was a castle of shadows and secrets mirroring Hamlet's mind. Winding up and down staircases, the camera kept returning to two locations, the throne room and Gertrude's bedroom. Olivier's adviser on the film was Ernest Jones, a psychoanalyst who had trained under Freud.

Q Compare Olivier's interpretation of the mother-son relationship with Mel Gibson's and Kenneth Branagh's. Which do you prefer and why?

Q Trace through Hamlet's relationship with Gertrude. How do you 'read' the mother-son relationship?

Hamlet's General Attitude to Women

'[F]railty thy name is woman' (1.2.146).

With the foundation myth of Eve tempting Adam to sin, Christianity has maintained a view that women are morally 'frail' and dangerously seductive to men. Women's sexuality has been, and still is, demonised as somehow intrinsically evil in many parts of the world. Appalling injustices have been committed against women and untold mischief done to communities because of this misogynistic view of human relationships ('misogyny' means hatred of women). Hamlet demonstrates a generalised disgust for women's vanity and moral 'frailty'.

Hamlet may feel betrayed by two women but he extends his criticism to the vanity and flippant approach to life of women in general in three scenes, which you should remember:

1   '[F]railty thy name is woman' (1.2.146).

2   'I have heard of your paintings too, well enough...' (3.1.137-40).

3   'Now get you to my lady's chamber...' (5.1.163-5). The image of mortality overcoming vanity was well known in Shakespeare's time.

The Players' Portrayal of Sexual Deception and Lust

It's a mark of Shakespeare's understanding of the way theatre can create powerful illusions, I think, that he takes the opportunity of a play-within-the-play to strengthen the audience's belief in the reality of Gertrude and Ophelia as living characters. Gertrude sits with Claudius, noticing that he's getting edgy as the play progresses. Ophelia is trying to cope with Hamlet making obscene suggestions to her every time she makes a comment. They are presented to us as women involved in love and sexuality — whereas we know immediately that the Player 'Queen' is a female stereotype, mouthing exaggerated lofty ideas about love and faithfulness that don't match up with the way humans really are.

Read the stage directions for the *Dumb Show* (3.2) and think about what the Queen's 'passionate action' looks like. Then consider what Gertrude's tone of voice is when she answers Hamlet's question, 'Madam, how like you this play?'. Is she amused, or bored, not really paying attention, or just commenting on a not very attractive idea when she says, 'The lady doth protest too much methinks'? In other words, it's nothing like the behaviour of a real woman so she doesn't take it personally.

Issues to Develop

Q It's important to think of Gertrude and Claudius as loving each other as well as being just sexual. Why? (Partly because it makes us realise that you can love someone else after losing a beloved partner, but there are other reasons too.)

The Relationship Between Thought and Action

Hamlet is a trained student — a thinker, and, as such, usually thinks things through and articulates ideas, trying to formulate logical responses to situations that perplex him. However, after the ghost has communicated with him (2.5), he feels the urgent need to stop using his mind so much and be active as a revenger. This sets up a **fundamental conflict between thought and action for Hamlet which is clearly seen in the soliloquies.**

Look closely at how these develop this conflict using these notes below.

- **Soliloquy 1:** ('O that this too too solid flesh would melt...' 1.2.129+) Hamlet expresses grief for his father's death and revulsion at his mother's speedy remarriage to father's brother. Despair is fed by his memories: 'Let me not think on it...', yet he does go on thinking, unable to even talk about his bitterness openly, let alone act against what's done.

- **Soliloquy 2:** ('O all you host of heaven!...' 1.5.92+) After the ghost's information, Hamlet's memory will focus his thoughts only on revenge. In an emotional frenzy, he writes down his discovery about uncle Claudius being a villain. This is his first action.

- **Soliloquy 3:** ('O what a rogue and peasant slave am I...' 2.2.502+) After watching the actor perform with such commitment that he made himself weep, 'And all for nothing', Hamlet attempts to motivate himself by mocking and cursing his own lack of passionate action. A little nagging thought that his 'melancholy' might have exposed him to diabolical temptation restrains him — maybe the ghost is lying. He needs more proof before acting as revenger and is motivated to set up a play to reveal Claudius's guilt. Hamlet satisfies himself that he's doing something at last.

- **Soliloquy 4:** ('To be or not to be...' 3.1.56+) Contemplating suicide and 'the dread of something after death', Hamlet accepts that 'conscience does make cowards of us all'. We make an emotional decision to do something and then the mind kicks in to prevent us. As Hamlet puts it, 'the native hue of resolution / Is sicklied o'er with the pale cast of thought'. 'Conscience' means that sense of knowing instinctively what's right and wrong, and suicide out of despair is doing a terrible wrong. This is a fundamentally serious point for Hamlet — again he has thought himself out of acting.

- **Soliloquy 5:** (''Tis now the very witching time of night...' 3.2.349+) Hamlet chooses the violent imagery of revenge, '...now could I drink hot blood', but lets us know that he intends to 'speak daggers to [his mother] but use none'. His high level of conflict is revealed in the distinction he makes between two 'hypocrites' in himself.

Without killing his mother, he will make his *tongue* only *say* to her what his *soul* is prompting him to actually *do*: send her sinful body and soul to punishment. Look at 3.4 to see how he struggles to maintain control of his deliberate 'hypocrisy'. He both does and doesn't want to harm her. His distress is so intense and physical that it requires another appearance of the ghost to shock him back to sense psychologically and to redirect his vengeful intentions towards Claudius.

- **Soliloquy 6:** ('Now might I do it pat, now a is a-praying…' 3.3.73+) One reason why Hamlet loses control so violently with Gertrude in 3.4 may be because he chooses to forego a near-perfect opportunity to take revenge on Claudius moments before. Claudius was alone, off guard, but *praying*. Again, thinking has stymied action for Hamlet. Why? He knows that his own father's soul is suffering in purgatory, killed when unprepared spiritually for death, '…with all his crimes broad blown'. If Hamlet takes revenge and kills Claudius 'in the purging of his soul', then Claudius will go straight to heaven, not a very satisfactory act of revenge. He wants to make sure that Claudius will go to hell permanently. Is this technically 'revenge' any more?

- **Soliloquy 7:** ('How all occasions do inform against me…' 4.4.32+) After discussing Fortinbras' war plan with a Norwegian soldier and understanding its cruel futility, Hamlet wonders why 'honour' alone (which drives Fortinbras) isn't sufficient to get him motivated to accomplish his 'dull revenge'. Once again he's thinking about reasons for not acting. He recalls crimes done to his family, resolving to cultivate only 'bloody' thoughts in future. The question remains, how far will thoughts take him into action?

There is a critical moment in the play when Hamlet is caught in an intensely emotional situation and acts spontaneously, mentally 'off guard'. He then makes a terrible mistake and kills Polonius (3.4). Instead of analysing the situation before springing into action, Hamlet simply reacts. This misguided and rash *reaction* has dire, unforeseen consequences. It leads directly to his immediate banishment to England, Ophelia's suicide and Laertes' return as a completely committed old-style revenger, which precipitates the murderous conclusion to the play.

In another context that is ambiguous, Hamlet declares 'there is nothing either good / or bad but thinking makes it so' (2.2.239-40). He knows that Rosencrantz and Guildenstern are trying to pump him for information but he may believe this as a fundamental truth.

Q What do you think Hamlet means by this statement? Look up the scene and see if you think he is serious or ironical. Do you think there is evidence from other incidents or statements that would indicate that Hamlet does believe thinking is so powerful?

Q In your view, does Hamlet ever take decisive and effective action?

Madness and 'antic disposition'

This theme deals specifically with perceived mental states of characters in *Hamlet*. Generalised statements about what drives ordinary people crazy in the real world just demonstrate the futility of trying to discover absolutes when it comes to understanding the workings of the human mind in distress. Polonius tries to define madness and gets caught up in his own rhetoric, reducing it all to a heartless and lame joke (2.2).

Hamlet charts the struggle of several individual minds to stay sane and collected in cruel circumstances. The picture is complicated by Hamlet when he tells his friends that he plans to act mad, 'to put an antic disposition on' (1.5.172) in order to secure a degree of personal safety while he plans how to work his revenge on Claudius.

You must discover for yourself when you think Hamlet is pretending and when he is truly out of control. You might come to the same conclusion as W.S. Gilbert in his skit *Rosencrantz and Guildenstern* (1895): 'Hamlet is idiotically sane with lucid intervals of lunacy'.

Hamlet chooses to act deranged in two ways, at least:

1 The 'Revenger' figure in plays known to Shakespeare's audiences followed a classical tradition of assumed madness and Hamlet continues this character type. Playing crazy gave the revenger a slight advantage, provided he acted credibly, in that he couldn't be held accountable for mouthing dangerous suspicions in public or making errors in the pursuit of his revenge (like accidentally killing the wrong person). The villain couldn't attack him in public because everyone assumed he was mad. Hamlet 'plays mad' in his most dangerous public scene at the Play and immediately afterwards (3.2).

2   Hamlet enjoys embarrassing people set to spy on him. Unlike other contemporary revenger-types, he creates diversions to release tension and make a savage game the audience can enjoy with him. This is the 'antic disposition' wordplay with Polonius, then Rosencrantz and Guildenstern (2.2), heard again when Rosencrantz and Guildenstern search for the body (4.2, 4.3). Sometimes he's flirting with hysteria by being deliberately cruel, as in bawdy insinuations to Ophelia and his mother in the 'Play' scene, while taunting Claudius. Next, he baits Rosencrantz and Guildenstern about playing recorders, then Polonius gets a final serve of malicious wit (3.2). His disrespect to Polonius's body (3.4) and cunning responses to Claudius (4.3) also suggest an 'antic disposition' shading dangerously into hysteria.

Is Hamlet ever truly mad? I don't think so, although he is subject to intense emotional distress in several scenes. Ophelia reports his deranged appearance and behaviour to Polonius (2.2), who immediately leaps to the partially correct conclusion that Hamlet is 'mad for [her] love, a lunacy' precipitated by his own strict instructions to deny herself to her would-be lover.

Q Look closely at Ophelia's description of Hamlet. How would you interpret the way he looked and acted in her presence?

Hamlet is overwrought but still sane in the 'nunnery' scene (3.1) even though Ophelia is left grieving for 'that noble and most sovereign reason...Blasted with ecstasy' (3.1.151-4). Claudius, emerging from hiding with Polonius, sees immediately that 'what [Hamlet] spake...was not like madness', even though Polonius stubbornly maintains that his own diagnosis is the correct one. Later in the 'closet' scene (3.4) a similar pattern of confusing behaviour emerges. Hamlet is distressed to the edge of hysteria after killing Polonius. He turns violently on Gertrude, leading her to exclaim 'alas he's mad' when he suddenly leaves off to converse with a ghost she can't see. This time Hamlet denies her the easy option of choosing to believe he's crazy: 'Lay not that flattering unction to your soul / That not your trespass but my madness speaks' (3.4.146-7). And she believes him. Later, she protectively covers Hamlet's outbreak when he picks a fight with Laertes at Ophelia's grave (5.1) by informing onlookers that his behaviour is 'mere madness', a passing fit.

Ophelia as 'a document in madness'

Ophelia goes spectacularly insane, 'Divided from herself and her fair judgement' (4.5.84) and drowns because, as Gertrude puts it, she is 'incapable of her own distress' (4.7.178). Read her mad scene and work out how everything she says makes 'sense', her 'thoughts and remembrance fitted', even though her reason has gone.

Reality and Illusion

This theme explores the uncertainty of human perception and the difficulty of knowing who and what to trust. What is reality? Only what you can see and understand with knowledge gleaned from your physical senses? Can aspects of human reality exist in unseen/unseeable spaces and ways of feeling? Hamlet certainly thinks so, as his soliloquies reveal. Belief in a supernatural reality beyond everyday life is still a reality for many people, even if it is not as widespread as it was in Shakespeare's time.

A key point of argument centres on the ghost of Old Hamlet. The murder victim who reappears to a living relative demanding vengeance is a stock figure of classical revenge theatre. Apparitions traditionally offer warnings or want to ensure that a task is fulfilled. In Shakespeare's time the appearance of a ghost was ambiguous for religious reasons. Not doubting that it had come from the afterlife, the question was, had it come from heaven or hell? Was it a devil out to ensnare a living soul in the guise of a loved relative? Alternatively, was it just a figment of a melancholic imagination in certain cases? Or could it be a sign of deeper social malaise, as Horatio suggests: 'This bodes some strange eruption to our state' (1.1.69)?

Horatio begins sceptically, as Marcellus reports with 'Horatio says 'tis but our fantasy' (1.1.23). However, he then sees, and instantly accepts, that the appearance of a ghost has a connection with some reality which is as yet unknown but that obviously needs to be revealed, 'a mote it is to trouble to mind's eye' (1.1.112). After his initial burst of excitement at having his suspicions verified by the ghost, Hamlet knows he must exercise caution until he has 'grounds / More relative than this' (2.2.556-7). Confirmation comes in Claudius's guilty reaction to the *Mousetrap* play, after which Hamlet declares, 'O good Horatio, I'll take the ghost's word for a thousand pound' (3.2.260-1).

Critics who argue about Hamlet's state of mind and treat the ghost as though it is a personal delusion tend to underplay the fact that three others see it as well, quite independently of him. Nonetheless, its appearances raise an issue relating to Hamlet's unstable mental state. How many times does the ghost actually appear, and why can't Gertrude see it in 3.4 when it was apparent to everybody in Act 1? Is it really there any more? Gertrude is adamant that she sees 'nothing at all, yet all that is I see' (3.4.132) when Hamlet 'bend[s his] eye on vacancy' (3.4.116).

Seeming and being: Another expression of this theme occurs in 1.2 when Gertrude asks her son, after he's agreed with her that everybody has to die some day, 'If it be / Why seems it so particular with thee?' (1.2.74-5). Hamlet explodes into a scornful retort to her offensively shallow suggestion that his 'show' of grief is put on. 'Seems madam? nay it is, I know not seems' (1.2.76). The gist of his counterattack is that if she thinks he's acting a part for show, like a player, she's only reading the surface of his grief.

Premonition of death — 'we defy augury': Just before the final duel with Laertes, Hamlet's short speech to Horatio about being prepared for death, whenever it might come, is prefaced by a slight but definite sense of foreboding. Hamlet shudders, conscious of 'how ill all's here about [his] heart...It is but foolery, but it is such a kind of gaingiving as would perhaps trouble a woman' (5.2.186-9). Here he seems to be accepting the kind of sensitivity to a premonition of danger a woman might be more likely to heed than a man, some feeling that exists in the space between reality and illusion. Unlike Horatio, who immediately says, 'If your *mind* dislike anything, obey it' [my emphasis], Hamlet seems to be beyond needing to pin the feeling down as something rational. It hasn't come from his mind any more but from his heart.

Q Is Hamlet correct to want to distinguish between 'seeming' and 'being' in the first 'court' scene (1.2), where there is so much hypocritical 'seeming' in his view?

Q Further explore Hamlet's attempts to distinguish between 'seeming' (illusion) and 'being' (reality).

Q List all the ways Hamlet himself uses 'seeming' and note his purposes for doing so. (See **Theatre and Life** (following) and **Madness and 'antic disposition'** (pp.61-3) to help you.

Theatre and Life

In 1956, Erving Goffman, a sociologist interested in human communication, wrote an influential book called *The Presentation of Self in Everyday Life*. Goffman drew on the language of stage performance to analyse the structure of social encounters in everyday life, using terms like following cues, rehearsal, mistiming, belief in your part, dramatic realisation and so on. It was a brilliant connection to make, but not an original one. Just go back to Shakespeare constructing a character who watches himself watching his world, speaking off the page to readers, playing his role carefully to stay alive.

'All the world's a stage and all the men and women merely players', says a melancholy character in another Shakespeare play, Jaques from *As You Like It*. In another play, Richard II says, just before he's murdered, 'Thus play I in one person many people, / And none contented' (*Richard II*, 5.5.31-2). Shakespeare and his contemporaries frequently used the metaphor of theatre and play-acting to express ideas about the vanity, folly and nobility of human activity.

The play-within-the-play within…?

Similarities between two interwoven ideas of acting a part in a play and performing a role in real life are explored repeatedly in *Hamlet*. Although Revenge Tragedy commonly contains a play-within-the-play, nowhere else do the characters become so obsessively involved with 'theatre' as a deep metaphor for their own and other people's behaviour.

In Soliloquy 3 Hamlet draws a distinction between stage acting, 'a fiction…a dream of passion' and his own impulse to act out his revenge (2.2.502-58). Since actors have turned up at Elsinore, he decides to enlist their help to put on a special piece of theatre designed to test both Claudius and the ghost's story. He has 'heard / That guilty creatures sitting at a play / Have by the cunning of the scene / Been struck…to the soul …' (2.2.541-4). Something about theatre connects with real life — it can affect people profoundly.

Hamlet develops this idea in his pre-show talk to the actors. Playing is seen as a kind of sacred activity, 'to hold…the mirror up to nature; to show…the very age and body of the time his form and pressure' (3.2.18-20). He's making the point for the benefit of the Globe audience, or you and me, the readers of the words on the page. The idea is: 'Listen up. Plays can teach you to look more thoughtfully at your own life and world'.

Within the world of the play, characters perform in different ways when they know they are 'on show' or are forced to play parts unfamiliar or repugnant to them. Think about the following:

- showing courtly 'actors' how professionals do it (2.2,and *Mousetrap* 3.2)
- 'seeming' Hamlet distinguishes between grief as 'actions that a man might play', with costumes and fake emotions, and the real thing 'within which passes show' (1.2.84-5)
- 'antic disposition' as Hamlet's virtuoso performance work (2.1, 2.2, 3.2, 4.2, 4.3)
- the 'nunnery' scene as a 'staged' event. Who's directing? Are all actors willing? (3.1)
- the 'closet' scene as a partly rehearsed scene that goes wrong for the director, Polonius (3.4)
- the 'graveyard' scene, virtuoso performance of wits, then a 'staged' ceremony that reveals its director's (Claudius) inadequate preparation (5.1)
- Hamlet mimicking Osric, whose living character in the Danish court is entirely a staged 'performance' (5.2)
- 'Duel' scene, performance of execution. Again, director Claudius loses control of his actors (5.2).

The Realities of Life and Death

Hamlet is a tragedy and must inevitably deal with how death comes to characters. There is no point trying to handle this theme with kid gloves or pretend that the plot is less brutal or confronting than it actually is. Hamlet continues to interest us because he is so obviously death-obsessed while also being intensely clever, involved with people and ideas, and alert to the precious richness of being alive. His journey of discovery opens a path for us to trace, through the relative psychological safety of drama, 'in a fiction, in a dream of passion' (2.2.504).

World religions and philosophies offer road maps for the human journey.

In Shakespeare's time English people found consolation and purpose in Christianity. Church rituals mapped out the beginning and end of life, from a baby's symbolic washing and protective anointing at baptism to proper burial of the dead body, during which the soul was cleansed and protected for its ongoing journey into the afterlife.

The importance of ritual processes is evident in *Hamlet*. The ghost's distress at being murdered is intensified because he died without proper religious preparation (1.5). Another example occurs at Ophelia's brief funeral (5.1), where the priest gets into an argument with Laertes. He defends himself by claiming that 'her death was doubtful'. Suicides were outcasts, damned for ending their own lives before their allotted time, so it would 'profane the service of the dead', argues the priest, to give Ophelia's body the full protective blessing. Knowing more about Ophelia's madness and death, we feel sorrow for her crushed spirit and share Laertes' passionate rage against a 'churlish priest' who's determined to go by the book.

Q Trace the deep significance of ritual processes in *Hamlet*.

In my opinion, the 'revenge ethic' is an historical phenomenon which now flies in the face of human respect for life. The essential dilemma raised by revenge killing is whether consciously choosing to end one's own or someone else's life, even for a very good reason, can ever be justified at all. You will find though that this is still very much an issue to be debated. Does revenge escalate violence or does it bring about a just solution?

The play, in fact, proposes two different and conflicting responses to retribution (repayment), and both are articulated by the ghost. On one hand, the ghost demands blood satisfaction, physical revenge on Claudius — Hamlet must be judge and executioner. In the very same speech, the ghost warns Hamlet not to injure Gertrude but to 'leave her to heaven' (1.5.86), which means leaving her to a combination of her own conscience and divine judgement to 'resolve' the matter for her.

The corrosive tension in Hamlet's personality stems from the appalling task handed to him in the first act: 'The time is out of joint: O cursèd spite, / That ever I was born to set it right' (1.5.188-9). In Soliloquy 7 (4.4) he wonders if it's cowardice holding him back from killing Claudius, and decides not. A few scenes earlier he has killed Polonius, expressed repentance for getting the wrong person but justified his action as part of a divine purpose working itself out through him (3.4). Later, he tells Horatio that he feels no remorse for sending Rosencrantz and Guildenstern to their deaths in England, because they meddled in politics (5.2).

Issues to Develop

- What is Claudius up to when he makes that long speech to Hamlet about 'death of fathers' in 1.2.86-117? Do you agree with his argument at all? Is he saying the same thing as Gertrude in her earlier speech 'Thou knows't 'tis common, all that lives must die' (1.2.72)?

- Examine the conversation between the gravediggers and then with Hamlet. Pinpoint issues being raised about life and death (5.1).

- Do you think that death through revenge is condoned in the play *Hamlet*?

SAMPLE QUESTIONS

1 'After all the famous speeches, *Hamlet* is finally just another story about crime and punishment.' Do you agree?

2 Is Hamlet the only tragic character in the play?

3 'At first, Hamlet puts on his 'antic disposition' but later he becomes really deranged.' Discuss.

4 'The flowers Ophelia gives and the songs she sings in 4.5 are more than a madwoman's ramblings: they work dramatically to remind an audience of both the accumulated sorrows that have driven her crazy and moral flaws in other characters.' Discuss.

5 Discuss the significance of the two female characters, Gertrude and Ophelia. In your view, are they classic victims in the male-dominated revenge plot or has Shakespeare made more dramatic use of them?

6 What makes it difficult for Hamlet to make up his mind? Should he act out his revenge or is his delay understandable?

7 'Hamlet's philosophical musings on death in 5.1 unite an audience in a strong bond of common humanity.' Do you agree?

8 How effective is the idea of theatre as a metaphor for human life?

9 'In life '…there is nothing either good or bad but thinking makes it so' says Hamlet to Rosencrantz (2.2.239-40).' True or false?

10 In *Hamlet* Shakespeare shows that pursuing revenge as a way of righting past wrongs only leads to the tragic destruction of innocent people.

11 The play shows that thinking undermines the ability to act and leads not only to procrastination but also to tragedy.

12 'In *Hamlet* we see that it is guilt rather than a clear conscience that drives people to do the right thing.' Discuss.

REFERENCES & READING

Text

Shakespeare, William, *Hamlet Prince of Denmark,* Philip Edwards (ed.), Cambridge University Press, Cambridge (2003).

References & Further Reading

Listed here are a few books and films that I've found useful. They all contain bibliographies to help you take your own research interests further.

Bullough, Geoffrey, *Narrative and Dramatic Sources of Shakespeare (1957-73)*, Vol VII, Routledge and Paul, London (1973). (SaxoGrammaticus story, the basis for *Hamlet*.)

McEvoy, Sean, *Shakespeare. The Basics*, Routledge, London (2000). (A good general introduction for starters.)

Ideas on the play

Brown J.R. & Harris, B., *Hamlet, Stratford-upon-Avon Studies 5*, Arnold, London (1965). (A stimulating collection of essays.)

Drakakis, John (ed.), *Alternative Shakespeares,* Methuen, London and New York (1985). (See Chapter 5.)

Jacobi, Derek, 'Hamlet' in R. Sales, (ed.) *Shakespeare in Perspective,* Ariel Books: BBC, London (1982), pp.186-92.

James, Clive, *Hamlet*, in R. Sales, (ed.) *Shakespeare in Perspective,* Ariel Books: BBC, London (1982), pp.179-85.

Jump, John (ed.), *Hamlet Casebook*, Macmillan, London (1968). (Good collection of significant approaches to play to get you thinking. Contains Jones essay *'Hamlet and Oedipus'*, pp.51-63.)

Showalter, Elaine, 'Representing Ophelia: women, madness and the responsibilities of feminist criticism', in P. Parker & G. Hartman, (eds), *Shakespeare and the Question of Theory*, Methuen, New York (1985), Chapter 5, pp.77-94.

Other Resources

Atwood, Margaret, *Good Bones and Simple Murders*, Doubleday, New York (1994). (See her poem 'Gertrude Talks Back'.)

The Play in Performance Beckerman, Bernard , *Shakespeare at the Globe*, (1962).

Brown, John Russell, *Shakespeare's Plays in Performance,* (1966).

Gurr, Andrew, *The Shakespearean Stage* (1970).

Gurr, Andrew, *Playgoing in Shakespeare's London* (1987).

Holmes, Martin, *The Guns of Elsinore* (1964).

Reynolds, George F., *Hamlet at the Globe*, Shakespeare Survey IX (1956), pp.49-53. A bit old-fashioned but still useful for speculations about staging the play on the original Globe stage space.

Thomson, Peter, *Shakespeare's Theatre* (1983). Good background on Shakespeare's company, stage features and performance ideas.

See Chapter 6, 'Hamlet and the actor in Shakespeare's theatre (pp.114-41).

Film and Video Material

Gamlet (Grigori Kozintsev, 1964). Russian version of *Hamlet* starring Innokenti Smoktunovsky as Hamlet.

Hamlet (Michael Almereyda, 2000). Modern day adaptation starring Ethan Hawke as Hamlet.

Hamlet (Kenneth Branagh, 1996) starring Kenneth Branagh as Hamlet. Comes in two versions, the complete 242 minutes version or a condensed version that runs for about two and a half hours.

Hamlet (Franco Zeffirelli, 1990) starring Mel Gibson as Hamlet.

Hamlet (Tony Richardson, 1969) starring Nicol Williamson as Hamlet.

Hamlet (Bill Colleran and John Gielgud, 1964) starring Richard Burton as Hamlet.

Hamlet (Laurence Olivier, 1948) starring Laurence Olivier as Hamlet.

Rosencrantz And Guildenstern Are Dead (Tom Stoppard) a play developed from the viewpoint of the two characters acting in a stage performance of *Hamlet*. Very witty if you know *Hamlet*. Stars Gary Oldman as Rosencrantz and Tim Roth as Guildenstern.

Reviews and Articles on Film Versions

Almereyda, Michael, (screenplay), *William Shakespeare's Hamlet*, (2000). The version starring Ethan Hawke, who writes Introduction to this screenplay.

Branagh, Kenneth, *Hamlet Screenplay*, see 'Introduction and Film Diary' (1996).

Corliss, Richard, 'Wanna Be...or Wanna Not Be?', review of Zeffirelli/ Mel Gibson/Glenn Close version, *Time Magazine*, January 21, 1991, p.48. (Zeffirelli's aim, says Corliss, 'is to make *Hamlet* so vigorous that the kids will forget it's poetry...The rest is violence'.)

Dent, Alan (ed.), *Hamlet: The Film and the Play* (1948). (An illustrated account of Sir Laurence Olivier's film version.)

Donaldson, Peter S., *Shakespearean Films/Shakespearean Directors*. Chapter 2 'Olivier, Hamlet and Freud'. (Close reading and discussion of film.)

Jorgens, Jack, *Shakespeare on Film* (1977) Chapter 14, 'Laurence Olivier's *Hamlet*'. (Comments on the film as 'Oedipal cinepoem', with a Freudian 'castle of inner experience' and 'Like Hamlet, the camera is on a quest for a meaningful pattern'.)

notes

CPSIA information can be obtained at www.ICGtesting.com
Printed in the USA
LVOW082037211111

255881LV00001BA/3/P